# women
# entre-
# pre-
# neurs

We Are Brave

# women entre- pre- neurs

## We Are Brave

**14 INSPIRING STORIES**

**Women Entrepreneurs Who Conquered Fear, Self-doubt, and Adversity to Build the Business of Their Dreams**

........................................................................................

## ellen smoak
**WITH 13 CONTRIBUTING AUTHORS**

Ashley Wainscott · Christin Menendez · Corina Frankie · Deborah Whitby
Deborah Yager · Dr. Denise Simpson · Diana Kundrotaite · Karla Rodriguez Lita Vallis
Rachel Brownlow Lund · Rachel Zierzow · Dr. Rose Anne Mulligan · Tiffani Marroquin

## WOMEN ENTREPRENEURS VOLUME 1: WE ARE BRAVE

Content Editor: Cynthia Guidici
Cover and Interior Design: Secia Zappitielli | Zapp Design

**the
society
of women
entrepreneurs.**

SocietyofWE.com | @societyofwe ⓘ ƒ 𝕏 | #weare

**MEDIA + SPEAKING:** Please contact media@societyofwe.com

**PUBLISHING:** For book publishing opportunities, contact
publishing@societyofwe.com

**ALL INQUIRIES:** support@societyofwe.com

# dedication

This book is dedicated to you, the brave woman entrepreneur.

We see you . . .
We believe in you . . .
And we are so glad you're here.

# table of contents

# introduction

## THE SOCIETY OF WE

When the urge of entrepreneurship calls to you deep from within, it's a very hard signal to ignore. First, you'll start thinking about your concept incessantly. Then it can start to feel like your current job, business, or life path is less interesting by the day. The idea to create your vision brews strong in your head, and it starts to feel like your only option is to make your idea a reality.

But what happens if you feel entirely sideswiped and knocked off your path? What if your best friend discourages you from pursuing your big idea and tells you to play it safe? What if the people you trust the most plant doubt in your mind? What happens when "logic" starts to kick in, and it feels safer and easier to stay where you are? Or most disruptive, what happens when your personal life takes a big turn? The surprise breakup, the health hurdles, the death of someone you love, or just an overall feeling that a bomb has gone off in your life?

**We've all that moment when it seems like the odds are stacked against us.**

Then what? How do you create from that place? How do you energetically rebound to find your place of inspiration again?

**What you're holding in your hands is a vault of wisdom from 14 female entrepreneurs who have forged ahead in their businesses, even in the face of the most challenging circumstances.**

9

Whether you're an aspiring entrepreneur trying to bring a dream to life or a seasoned business owner looking for inspiration to play a bigger game and be reminded that you're not the only one that has emotionally brutal seasons of life, this book is for you.

If you're a woman reading while in the conception phase, we know how fragile an idea can feel when you're just getting a new concept off the ground. Whether you're finally going to open a health practice, start selling your art collection, start a coffee company, create an app, or pursue a freelance consulting career, this book will show you that **it's all possible as long as you never, ever give up.**

Whatever dream you're setting out to create, this book will serve as a fountain of wisdom and knowledge to help you withstand the challenging stages of bringing a business to life. We want you to find comfort in knowing that you're not the only one who's questioned your entire existence and worth as a woman while following a dream many people in your life may not ever fully understand.

If you're a woman who has already taken the huge leap of faith to choose the path of entrepreneurship for the long run, this book is loaded with truth and insight for you. We hope that you read these pages and have a feeling of "me too," as the authors of this book share their hearts and souls with you. Continuing to choose the rollercoaster of entrepreneurship is a path we understand intimately, and we deeply admire your commitment.

. . . . .

***Women Entrepreneurs Volume I: We Are Brave* is a collaboration book stories by 14 brave business owners inside The Society of Women Entrepreneurs who have persevered in the face of tremendous hardship, roadblocks, and unwanted life surprises.** From seven-figure earners to women who recently chose radical career shifts, one thing unites us all: We all have a story to tell. Each of these stories has been thoughtfully and vulnerably written to leave you filled with what you need most to succeed: courage, bravery, guts, and a whole lot of grit. We're here to share the most authentic parts of our hearts with you, to remind you that you're not alone on this journey.

Together, we spent six months in sisterhood, writing this book and carefully crafting a message that will touch you to the core of your heart. It will leave you feeling *"Yes, I can do this. I can pick up all the tiny pieces and rebound. Yes, I can create the life and business my soul craves most."*

**We believe that women entrepreneurs are the future of humanity and that you, the reader, matter.** Your ideas matter. Your calling matters. Your emotional sanity throughout the process matters.

Pour yourself a hot cup of tea and prepare to settle into our cozy living room with the 14 new "sister friends" whom you're about to meet. We've shared our truth with you as we would with a best friend. We've shared our hearts with you like a blood sister would. We share our knowledge with you as a true ally in entrepreneurship.

Feel free to read this book from beginning to end order or flip open a page to leave it up to the universe to choose the perfect dose of story medicine for you today.

It is our greatest wish that in each of these chapters you find some part of yourself in the author. That you believe in yourself a little more, acknowledge yourself a little more loudly, and take action a little more boldly.

Every single day you choose entrepreneurship is a massive win. Thank you, sister, for being here. Your journey to inspiration, growth, and sisterhood awaits.

# your life depends on this

**ELLEN SMOAK**

"The rest of your life depends on this." These were the words which woke me up that morning. It was only 3:33 a.m., two long weeks after my ex-fiancé and I broke up.

Up until that morning, I'd desperately cried myself to sleep every night. Just two weeks prior, my ex and I had been holding each other, crying on one another, and promising one another that we were going to be okay. We had been fighting for months, but I thought the fighting was finally coming to an end. I thought we'd pushed through our differences, healed our hurt, and made it through.

In short, I still thought we were going to be together forever.

"The rest of my life depends on what, exactly?" I asked myself. "Moving on? Getting over him? Or just getting out of bed tomorrow?" I tried to wrap my head around what Spirit was trying to tell me, but my mind was too tired to think. I lay there for another hour, just staring at the ceiling. The moonlight peeked in through the curtains, casting a faint glow in the room. Yet it felt like the darkest room I'd ever been in. I'd never felt so alone, so invisible, and so worthlessly discarded in my entire life.

"How did this happen? What could I have done differently? Why *me*?" I kept asking myself, over and over and over again. I'd quite literally never felt something so painful in my entire life, and the farther I went down my rabbit hole of shock and confusion, the deeper my anxiety and depression set in.

I closed my eyes again, holding back more tears. It was all I could do not to scream. I felt like I was dying in that bed without him. I closed my eyes even tighter and started to pray. "Spare me, or be done with me," I asked. I prayed to God, Spirit, The Universe, anyone and anything that could take away my pain. I just couldn't take anymore. "Help me understand why this was happening to me. Help me understand what this means. Help me know what I am supposed to do next with my life," I asked, over and over and over.

I prayed for what felt like another hour, as tears of pain and surrender streamed down my face. A few moments later, I felt a calm come over my body, as if the same spirit that had just spoken to me was now engulfing the room. My heart was still terribly broken, but I started to feel a sense of relief. A faint knowingness entered my mind. A knowingness that everything would, in fact, be okay. I opened my eyes one last time to take in the moonlight, then I drifted back to sleep.

• • • • •

Our breakup had been one of those slow, painful ones—the kind that started off as a simple blemish and ended up scarring our relationship for life. Shortly after getting engaged, we dived into our first business together as entrepreneurs, working long hours to build our company into one which could sustain us. It was 2008, right in the middle of the real estate crash. We'd both been in real estate separately for several years—I as a real estate agent, and he as a real estate investor. It was a grim season for real estate, as you can imagine. Most people in or around the industry were losing properties, paychecks, jobs, and incomes. He and his brother had been turned on to the property preservation industry—a very niche market inside the real estate industry in which banks and lenders hire local technicians to clean out, repair, and maintain homes after they go into foreclosure. As entrepreneurs, we saw the massive opportunity of a company of this kind at the time, and as real estate professionals, we felt grateful to have found something just to sustain us.

We quickly began buying trucks and hiring crews to service lenders throughout the southeast, contracting with Bank of America,

Countrywide, Fannie Mae, and Freddie Mac. The foreclosure market was booming, as were our incoming business leads. It wasn't the prettiest of work environments, however. We saw some really bad situations and devastating circumstances. I remember going to bed most nights just giving thanks to God that we were all okay, yet feeling tremendously sad for everyone affected by the crash.

Regardless, our business grew like crazy almost overnight, employing other family members and friends along the way. Working with my partner had been a dream of mine for most of my life. The idea of starting and scaling a family business really excited me, and we seemed to be on the same page of making that dream a reality. We spent our days working hard, our evenings playing with our adopted fur babies, and our nights together as a couple. Life was good. Really good. I was on top of the world, with my future in full sight. Little did I know, however, that life wasn't going to play out the way that I thought. I didn't know it at the time, but I was being prepared for something more—something that would take every ounce of strength, courage, and capacity to endure, yet would end up becoming a beautiful blessing, merging my past with my yet-to-be-seen destined future.

· · · · ·

Hard work had always been a way of life for me. Growing up, I saw both of my parents work tremendously hard. My mother was, and still is, an English teacher. She'd quit her demanding court reporting business when I was little to take on a career as an adult education English teacher, a career that granted her the ability to be present when my little brother and I got home from school. My dad always worked physically hard as the owner/operator of a mechanic shop, often coming home exhausted at the end of the day but still finding enough energy to bring excitement to our household. Throughout high school and college I always worked, often holding down two part-time jobs at once while completing my education.

Being raised by an English teaching mother had its developmental perks. When I was in elementary school, I started helping her grade her papers. Words, paragraphs, sentences, stories—I started falling in love with everything found on a page or inside of a book. My mother was also a consummate reader, devouring almost a book a day. She encouraged me to read as much as possible, though it was the writing and the authors themselves that interested me most.

To me, authors were superheroes, and their books the way they saved the world. I used to beg my mother to take me to the library, just so I could admire their faces on the bookshelves. I started dreaming about becoming an author and turning into a "super-hero" one day. I used to daydream about what it would be like to hold my own book in my hands, see my words in print, and sign the inside cover flap. I can remember staring out of the window each time my mother and I left a bookstore, visualizing what it would be like to write and publish a book. Even at that young age, I could see so clearly what my purpose was. Why I was put on this earth. I was supposed to write a book.

In high school, I dived heart-first into my English classes, especially enamored of a certain author who fascinated me most, namely, Pat Conroy. I devoured his books and wrote just about every paper on his dark and mysterious characters. In college, I nervously signed up for my first creative writing class during my junior year, unsure if I had what it took to come up with something to write about "out of thin air." I remember feeling terrified when I left class that first day, not even knowing where to start. I ended up sitting at a coffee shop until 2 a.m., writing furiously in my college-ruled notebook. I found myself going inward, contemplating and intuiting all at once. It was quite possibly the most alive and on purpose that I'd ever felt. I walked away the next day with an A on my manuscript, even further convinced to write my own book one day.

• • • • •

Following college, however, my book-writing dreams took a back seat to my desire to spread my wings. I left the South, moved west to San Diego, started a real estate career, and eventually began my first business as a nonprofit event planner. When the econom-ic crash of 2007 hit, however, both my real estate career and my budding business came crashing down, forcing me to start seeking other options. And as luck would have it, that's exactly when I met my fiancé, fell in love, and moved back to the South to be with him. I thought the rest of my life was planned. I was engaged, establish-ing a life and a new family business with my future husband. What could go wrong?

A year after getting engaged, after moving in together, adopting fur babies together, and building our seven-figure business together, I came home one evening to find my then-fiancé in a very strange emotional state. I couldn't tell what was wrong at first, but I could feel his strange and shifted energy deeply in every inch of my body. It was December 21, 2009, just two days before both sides of our family were driving in for the holidays to help us celebrate our first Christmas in our new home. I had just walked in the door after treating myself to a long, slow yoga class after spending the majority of the prior week prepping for our guests. New decorations, new Christmas china, new towels, sheets, and comforters—our new home was set. All except trimming the tree.

When I walked in from yoga that night at half past 9 o'clock, I noticed that my fiancé was already standing next to the Christmas tree, unpacking ornaments. When I walked over to start helping him, a strange feeling came over my body. Something was off. He was off. He was staring into a box of Christmas ornaments that his mother had passed down to him before she died. Just as he started to unwrap them, he said, "I don't want to get married anymore."

I looked down at the Christmas ornaments on the table. The newspaper they had been wrapped in was dated January 2006, the year that his ex-wife had walked out on him, 30 days before his mother died of cancer. Those Christmas ornaments had been wrapped up after their last Christmas together, and they'd hadn't been unwrapped since.

I cried myself to sleep that night. "The Night of the Ghost of Christmas Past," I called it. Something dreadful had come out of those wrapped up Christmas ornaments. Something that would forever haunt our soon-to-be-over engagement.

· · · · ·

We spent the next year and a half together trying to make our relationship work. He didn't want to be without me, but his fear of being married again kept us on a merry-go-round of emotions. One day we'd seem to be moving past his fear, only to have that "ghost" creep up again the next.

Instead of truly facing what was happening, I dived into my yoga practice. Hardly a day went by that didn't end on the mat. Yoga became my salvation. My peace. Though our business was doing well—exceptionally well—the pain I was experiencing in my heart from feeling so unwanted in my relationship was almost too much to bear. There were days when I just wanted to crumble and nights when I wanted to disappear. I turned to yoga, and then to writing about it, as a way to save my aching soul and soothe my tattered spirit.

In 2010, I started my first online blog. I began thinking about my life's journey in a deeper way and discovered a new passion for self-help and spiritual development. Thinking about and discerning my journey, self-help, and personal development became my new passions, and writing my new way to cope. My written journey of transformation through our painful, yet enlightening breakup ended up reaching hundreds of people online before our relationship was even over. Yet I still clung to the idea that we would somehow still be okay.

The better my blog did, the more interested I became in the online publishing niche. The worlds of blogging, content marketing, and online course creation were still relatively new back then, and online business opportunities were vast and wide open. I started learning everything I could about building an audience, creating content, and selling online courses to my readers. I started following as many people as I could, mostly internet marketers and self-help gurus who had millions of followers and raving fans. I devoured their newsletters, emails, and marketing strategies, soaking up anything and everything I could in preparation to follow suit.

Up until that point in my life, I'd mostly worked for or been an entrepreneur alongside someone else. My enthusiasm for all things business made me the perfect person to team up with. Partner with me, take advantage of my sales and marketing skills, and I'd take your business to the next level in a heartbeat. I jumped on board my first entrepreneurial journey with my best friend. Next, my fiancé. Being in business with other people felt safe. It had always been much easier for me to help someone else build their business dream than it was to venture off completely and fearlessly on my own. But Spirit had other plans. I didn't know it at the time, and it was the most gut-wrenching experience of my entire life, but my fiancé breaking up with me a few days before my birthday in June of 2012 would end up becoming the best thing that ever happened to me.

· · · · ·

When I woke up again later that hot summer morning, three weeks after our breakup, I couldn't immediately tell that something was different. I waited for the same desperate tears to stream down my face, but they didn't. A few moments later, I just about bounced out of bed. It was the first time since my breakup that I actually woke up feeling refreshed and renewed, as if a switch had been turned on inside me. I got dressed immediately, walked to my desk, opened my computer, and began to write.

My fingers moved across the keyboard with such fiery determination that I had to consciously slow down in order to make sense of what was being channeled through my fingertips. Several pages later, I stopped typing. I'd been in what felt like a trance for God only knows how long, and sitting right there on my computer screen was the outline of my very first book.

My days and nights turned into a super-charged vortex of creation, with me writing from the time the sun came up in the morning until well into the wee hours of the night. My mornings started with a quick cup of coffee on my porch before the South Carolina summer heat set in, and then I was back inside for the day, laboring through the birth of my first book baby. I wrote for close to 15 hours every single day, taking breaks only to eat, check my email, dance out my excitement, or take a walk outside to get some fresh air. Hundreds of hours, dozens of cups of coffee, and just 28 days later, I'd written an entire book.

*Breakups Are a Bitch, but Getting Over Them Doesn't Have to Be!* became the foundation for my new online business. I used that book to launch several online conferences, interviewing some of the biggest names in the personal development space. I took the content inside of the book and turned it into coaching programs and online courses. I used my knowledge of sales and marketing gained during previous entrepreneurial ventures to grow my audience into the tens of thousands, eventually reaching millions of people around the world.

. . . . .

Today, I lead and mentor thousands of other business women as the founder and CEO of The Society of Women Entrepreneurs. The "Sistership," as I like to call it. Since 2016, The Society of WE has been helping women start and scale their businesses by providing community, mentorship, and ongoing support. On any given day, one of our members and her business is being positively affected by the resources found inside our sisterhood. Had my engagement never ended, this vast and resourceful sisterhood may never have existed.

Looking back, I've finally come to understand what those words meant at 3:33 a.m. that hot summer night. I'd just spent the better part of three years in a relationship that hadn't been serving me. I'd fought to make it work, tried to fit myself into a life that wasn't meant for me, and put my own dreams on the back burner for long enough. "The rest of my life" depended on me digging deep inside myself to find my strength, heal my hurt, step into my power, and make my book writing dreams come true.

It's amazing to think about all our trajectories in life. Every experience, every person, every win, every loss—everything that's been put on your path is divinely and strategically placed there so that you can gain the insights and wisdom you need to become who you're meant to become in the world.

Like me, you've had situations that have shaped you, family members who've affected you, or even your own heartbreaks that have helped you along your path of becoming fully and completely YOU. I have yet to meet a woman entrepreneur who hasn't, at some point, come skidding into her business with scuffed knees, a bruised heart, and a slightly weathered, yet enlightened soul.

I have also yet to meet a woman entrepreneur who hasn't turned her life's pain into the power she needed to create something magical inside her business. You, my business sister, are no different. No matter what your journey has been up until now, and no matter where you are on your path, I see you, all of you, and I recognize you, fully.

My wish for you is that you also see yourself, all of you, and that you recognize yourself completely. Spirit knew exactly what she was doing when she gifted you the vision for your business. It's meant for you, and you only. Trust yourself and your inner wisdom to tell you what to do next. If you're stuck, ask for help. Ask your God, ask Mother Nature, ask whomever or whatever you believe in to show you the way. Often, there's something much bigger at play, something that, once you discover it, learn it, or are shaped by it, will make all the difference to you, your family, your business, and your life's work. The challenging experiences in your life are the ones that will ultimately transform a part of you that's necessary to become who you're truly meant to be in this world.

## APPLYING THE LESSONS

### 1. The power is in the surrender, not in the control.

If you're experiencing a challenge in your life, take note of how you might be trying to control its outcome. It may sound counter-intuitive, but "giving up" your challenges to a higher power is much more powerful than continuing to "fight" for what you want. Sure, you want to see a situation or a relationship end up a certain way, and having a guaranteed outcome may bring you a sense of relief, but are you holding on so tight to your desired outcome that a possible alternative doesn't have any room to present itself?

Tonight, before going to sleep, I invite you to surrender your challenges to a power up above through prayer. Ask your God to take your situation and fill it with love and light. Ask for clarity. Ask for peace. Most importantly, ask that your desire to control be shifted into a desire to see how God wants you to see, so that you can be who God wants you to be.

### 2. Keep the faith.

There's a reason that we pray from our knees: because we're often on them when we finally decide to ask for help. Whether you've been on your knees one, two, or a hundred times, what I want you to know is this: rock bottom is the strongest and best place to lay a new foundation. There's no way to build but back up.

You may or may not feel like you've ever hit rock bottom, but hard times can knock you down regardless. What I challenge you with today is to strengthen your faith in yourself and your desires, rather than let upset and challenge steal your faith.

### 3. Trust the process.

Have you ever looked back at a situation in your life and thought, *How did I get myself into that? Why did I put up with that for so long? What the heck was I thinking?* It's been said that we're all just spiritual beings having a human experience. And if we're going to learn our spiritual lessons and receive our spiritual gifts, then there's no way around the process but through it.

If this is the case, what can you glean from your human experience? What are the spiritual gifts that every difficult situation has had to offer you? Take inventory of these gifts. Write them down. Have you received the gift of patience? The gift of awareness? The gift of grace? Next, write down all the ways you can use your spiritual gifts during this "human experience" you're having right now. Make a commitment to embody your spiritual gifts and reflect them out in the world—especially in times of struggle. Embodying your spiritual gifts is like turning yourself into a crystal and placing yourself in direct sunlight: your beauty and light will fill every room you walk into.

The more you commit to living a spiritual life, the more insight, understanding, and inner peace you will experience along the way. These three things will help you wide and far—from having healthy relationships to staying in alignment with your entrepreneurial purpose. No matter what (or who) might be happening in your life right now, no matter where you've been, what you've lost, or who's shown up to challenge your belief in yourself along the way, remember this: your power is in the surrender, not in the control. Keep the faith, sweet sister, and trust the process. *Because the rest of your life really does depend on it.*

# hard breaks & new beginnings

## ASHLEY WAINSCOTT

"I'm leaving you." The three words I never thought I could say frantically launched themselves out of my mouth.

I sat there in fear as panic swallowed me. My hands were shaking, my body was sweating. I had rehearsed this situation over and over, yet I could not imagine what would come next. I could not move. My thoughts came screeching to the forefront of my mind. Now what? What is he thinking? Should I have said that? I had played out every scenario in my head but still felt unprepared.

The sheer courage it took to say those three words left me feeling empty. Tears and heartbreak filled the air. When there was nothing left to say, I got up and walked out of the house, shutting the door behind me, leaving the life I once knew. The life I had built. In that moment of feeling heartbroken and alone, it clicked that I had no idea what was next. Self-doubt swept over me. and I thought, "Did I just throw away my whole life?"

· · · · ·

I grew up as a goofy, wild, adventurous, and exceptionally bossy little girl who felt the need to always be the decision maker.

Shooting for the stars, my dreams were never too big for me. As I saw it, the sky was the limit. That was how I viewed everything in my life. When it came to decisions, I did not blink an eye. I knew exactly what I wanted. I was a strong, independent woman even as a little human learning to navigate life.

My freedoms and creativity were important to me throughout my childhood, teenage years, and even into my twenties. I thrived in an expressive environment, always signing up for organizations that allowed me to better myself. My hobby of dance frolicked through every phase of life with me. I had been on studio and school dance teams, exploring every type of dance style available. I enjoyed new opportunities and new facets of life. I cherished the creative freedoms my parents gave me early on. I was a creator.

My parents divorced when I was young, so I felt the need to start "adulting" earlier than most kids might. I matured quickly in life, always reaching for the stars. I was not going to wait around for life to happen to me. Life was going to happen because of me. I saw my parents still operating as a team, but also as strong, brave individuals who ran their lives separately from each other. This rooted in me.

Now let's talk about what led me to that heartbreaking scene you read earlier. I had built up my life in Austin and was going to school to get my degree in entrepreneurship. I was ready to take over the world, although I had taken on more than I could really handle, but this was not unusual in my special role as the over-achiever. Everything seemed fine.

· · · · ·

I was living a "normal" life according to society's standards. I was on track to checking all the boxes: go to college, find a good job, find a spouse, find a good place to live, and start a family. That's what adults do, right? You check off the "to do" items on the list, and then you're all set for life.

WRONG.

With so much going on in my personal life, I found it difficult to

notice my declining health and how it was related to the decisions
I had been making. I had so much vertigo I could barely walk.
I actually had vertigo spells during which I could not get out of
bed for days at a time. I would miss what seemed like weeks of
my life. I was also having frequent panic attacks. I remember, at
one point, I was leaving a college class on campus when a panic
attack hit. I was so alarmed I got in my car and drove myself
to the hospital. I was certain I was dying this time; it was different than the other attacks. Turns out, it was just another panic
attack.

This is when it all started to come crashing down. Over the next
few months, several close friends gave me concerned feedback
regarding my aura; something was off. Their feedback seemed
both coincidental and out of the blue, and these conversations
lingered in my head, eventually sparking me to do some reflection. Who was I? Where was I going with my life? What were my
hobbies? Did I have goals? What were they?

I didn't have answers to any of these questions. This was shock-
ing and hard to swallow at first. I felt like I was a stranger to myself. It took some time to digest, and after sitting with this lack of
clarity for months, I realized I felt dull about life and had lost my
sense of self. I had no idea who I was. Not only that, but I started
connecting all of my current physical symptoms and struggles
to this dark hole that was gaping inside of me. It occurred to me
that I had not paid any attention to this emptiness or checked in
with myself for years. What a big ol' mess!

I got so caught up in other people's ideals and standards of life,
my own desires and goals became foggy and almost obsolete.

The end result: I needed to be fully invested in myself to find
the answers to all those questions I had been asking myself. The
tricky thing was, if I did this, I was going to be the cause of hurt
and pain for other people. One of the biggest changes that I
would have to make would be ending my long-time relationship.
The breakup consisted of walking away from my current life on
a mission to reconnect with myself. I knew there would never be
a good time to do this, so I just chose a day in December and
decided to be brave. I broke off my relationship, kick-starting the

new "Journey of Me" (a.k.a. My Quarter-Life Crisis.)

· · · · ·

I walked out that door that day with a whirlwind of thoughts swirling through my head. As I walked to my car, I tried to grasp the decision I had made. I had to focus on putting one foot in front of the other. I started the engine and just sat there. And then the fear crept in. "What the fuck did I just do?" Full-on self-doubt hit me next, and wow, was it strong. Tears flowed down my cheeks. I cried until I couldn't cry anymore. Then this awakening swept over me: I was not going to spend one more moment thinking about this fear and doubt. I had made my decision. I put the car in drive, hit the gas, and drove away with a new emptiness in my gut that actually felt comforting.

I moved back home and lived with my parents while I figured my life out. I was ready to kick-start the Journey of Me, but I had no clue how to go about doing so. After some soul searching, I decided that the first step was to focus all my effort on loving myself: the good, the bad, and the ugly. I intended to channel that bossy little girl inside me who not only loved herself, but who also took control of her life.

For me, this was a rebirthing experience. Part of the process involved finding out the amount of anxiety that I carried around with me daily. I didn't even realize I had anxiety! I was in complete denial when my doctor told me his diagnosis. I laughed and told him that anxiety didn't sound like something I had, yet I knew nothing about anxiety. I was so sure that I did not have it until he presented the symptoms and facts. I walked out of the doctor's office with an equal mix of clarity and confusion. Apparently I had anxiety. This was one of the new health issues that arose as a result of my self-care deprivation. My body felt as if it had been beaten up. Everything was weighing on me so heavily that I felt physically exhausted.

First things first: therapy. I had gotten away from going to therapy as I entered my twenties. Throughout my childhood and early adulthood, however, therapy was a BIG part of my life. I have truly always enjoyed walking into a "safe" environment where I can state my honest and open opinions without judgment. My therapists have acted as guides who lead me through uncertainty, provide alternative perspectives, and help me see what I am saying.

The healing journey did not stop there. I had several friends and doctors recommend I look into acupuncture and yoga to help with my anxiety and general health needs. I didn't know much about either and was intimidated by the sound of them. I was willing to try anything, though. I ended up taking more of a holistic route and continued my healing journey through yoga and acupuncture for years. All of this felt foreign at first, but after a few months, I started to really feel a change.

While all of this was going on in my personal life, I was making a BIG change in professional career as well. I was transitioning from my corporate job into the event planning industry. As a little girl, my dream was to be one of two things when I grew up: a ballerina or a wedding planner. Since I was not a fan of tights (and their extreme level of discomfort), my hopes of being the ballerina were slim to none, so I became hyper-focused on becoming a wedding planner one day. I would picture myself dressed in a sleek ivory business suit with a bun and a headset— like J.Lo in the movie *The Wedding Planner.*

I would dream of ordering others around frantically, of flowers being rushed in every direction and of weddings going off without a hitch. Imagine my surprise, then, when I eventually learned that the job wasn't anything like what I had pictured. Turns out there's a lot more to planning a wedding than I'd thought. Some things in life just don't turn out as planned.

I started toying with the idea of going off on my own to start a business. I know . . . what was I thinking at a time like that? A little insane? Yep! I had fears, though. Like many, I was hesitant. I was unsure if I was ready to be vulnerable in such an unknown space. But in typical "Ashley fashion," I just jumped right in. I initially saw a gap in the construction industry, and it sparked further research.

When I realized I had found a hole in the market, I made it my mission to create a business that would solve the problems and frustrations that I had seen consumers deal with. I created a business that provided a simple, efficient process for homeowners needing make-ready services before selling their homes. The goal was not only to be a one-stop shop for clients, but also to weave important values, such as communication, honesty, reliability, and trust, into my process. I knew nothing about this line of work other than the biggest problems homeowners were facing with contractors. I had to learn how to bridge the gaps, turn that skill into a business process, provide a consistent service, and make a profit. On top of that, I was learning the basics of all the trades: plumbing, electrical, carpentry, drywall, painting, etc.

I started my home renovation firm, Simply Sold, with the goal of opening channels of communication and self-expression in the remodeling industry. One of my intentions was to create a company that promotes and encourages an empowering environment where employees, staff, and vendors can thrive. The other intention was to create empowering environments inside the homes of my clients so that they, too, can thrive. The combination of empowering my team and empowering my customers gives my business purpose on a daily basis. It's why we exist.

It occurred to me, while writing this chapter, that there's a connection between the energetic space I created in which to express myself after my breakup and the physical spaces that my company now creates for our clients to express themselves on a daily basis. This awareness made me realize how vital self-expression is to every individual and their inner peace. We all want to be heard. It's as simple as that.

Gaining self-awareness starts with listening to yourself. As you read earlier in my story, I thought I was limited. I was not listening to myself, which meant I had very little awareness of my own needs, and the only barrier I was facing was myself.

This self-discovery journey you have been reading lasted roughly a decade of my life. I am happy to report that I am on the other side of the fence now, but it took time and a great deal of trial and error. The key is to find your recipe for keeping yourself balanced. Don't give up!

Because I am now tuned into myself, I know my limits, my boundaries, my strengths, and my weaknesses. I have the confidence to be a leader. I am a rebel who inspires and hires other self-aware leaders who aspire to create change. I have a "better every day" attitude with a constant urge to grow and learn. I've made the changes in my life, and I have seen the results that can happen when you make these adjustments.

There are limitless journeys we can choose for our life. We are not confined to what we know or what we have seen. We can truly do anything. Use the action items below and the insights I've shared to see if they add even more vibrancy to your life. I encourage you to try! Trust the process and be you.

## APPLYING THE LESSONS

### 1. Meditate.

One of the most beneficial practices I have introduced into my lifestyle is meditating. I remember the first time I heard about meditation. I was watching *The Ellen DeGeneres Show*, and she was talking about her morning practice of mediation. At the time, I thought meditation was a strange, mysterious concept, and that could be what you are thinking, too. Once Ellen talked more about her personal experience with meditation, I was encouraged to sit down and try it out. It was awkward at first, but after some time, I eventually started to get it. My best advice is to download one the many available meditation apps to your phone and allow it to guide you through the meditation. Start small with three- or five-minute meditations and then graduate into longer periods of time, such as 10 or 15 minutes. I graduated to longer periods of time once I felt that it was becoming more natural for me and I was becoming comfortable sitting with the stillness. Start slow, and be patient with yourself. Most importantly, start to take note of how your moments in stillness are beginning to create positive changes in other areas of your life. Pay attention; you will see the results.

### 2. Build your self-awareness.

Once I started to understand how my mind was operating, I could stop and watch my thoughts roll by. Mediation is one form of getting in touch with your internal dialogue. You want to start understanding when you feel anxious, fearful, angry, or upset. All are emotions you can physically wear, which is what can weigh you down and cause physical illness. Let's agree that we all want to avoid that.

Listen to yourself and engage with that inner voice that you probably ignore every day. While you are listening to your inner voice, start to consider your self-care. How can you operate at your best? What are some self-care routines you've been wanting to implement but have been putting off for months or maybe even years? How much time do you set aside for yourself, and could you allocate more? Do not feel ashamed if your answer is less than ideal.

When I began to focus on self-care, I eased into it and only committed only to acupuncture and yoga. Now, I work out three times a week, go to acupuncture once a month, go to the chiropractor once a quarter, and get a deep tissue massage at least once a quarter. Not only that, but I have a morning routine that involves meditation, journaling, reading, stretching, positive affirmations, and goal setting. This routine sounds like it sucks up a lot of my time because it does. I am aware that without these practices in my morning routine and my monthly self-care rituals, I am not able to operate at my best. You will feel the difference, too.

## 3. Be Present.

My ability to stay present has saved me at times. Living in the moment and being present is key to moving in the right direction: forward. The past has already occurred, and the future has not happened yet, but you do have this moment right now. With all my past health problems, my new routines set me up to be more present in my day-to-day life.

I highly recommend the book *The Power of Now* by Eckhart Tolle for anyone who wants to dive deeper into these practices. This book took my "Now" to the next level.

## 4. Choose yourself.

One thing I realized along my journey is that choosing myself has been a key component to my success in both my personal and business life. Not only do you mind your own business more (and focus less on others), but you don't worry about things that are not in your control. You maintain your awareness in every moment. What's the downside to living in the moment and appreciating the moment you have right now? Nothing. Absolutely nothing.

• • • • •

All of these new ways of being have allowed me to continue to adapt and change with my business. You can't fight the transformation. Instead, live in the present and welcome the changes. Every phase of life will be that much easier. You will still have those hard hits from the unexpected, but their impacts can be measured on a smaller scale.

Practicing these steps has also led me to find a life that resonates with me more than ever. My capabilities continue to expand as I continue down a path of learning, forever learning. Taking these steps to honor yourself, and what you need will inevitably push you toward deeper enlightenment. Do the world a favor and be your best self. Embrace you for all that you are and allow the world to get to know you.

Now the real question is "Who are you going to become?"

# the hero's journey

## CHRISTIN MENENDEZ

It's November 27th, 1994, and I'm in my bedroom at my childhood home in Tampa, Florida. I'm a 10-year-old girl, eye to eye with a livid grown man who happens to be my stepfather, Rick. He's towering over me, clenching my jaw in his massive hand. His nose is pressed against mine, and he's yelling directly in my face, after having just punched holes through my door.

Only seconds earlier, my desperate plea to extend my bedtime had been denied, so I mouthed off to my parents about how unfair it was. I made sure to punctuate my sentiments by slamming and locking my bedroom door. Rick, a hot-tempered man with a zero-tolerance policy, had something to say about this dramatic display of defiance. He had put his fist through my door two or three times before I finally unlocked it, too scared of what might happen if I forced him to break down the entire door to get to me.

He's shouting, but his words don't register. I only know they're threatening and condescending—something about me being a disrespectful, ungrateful little shit, and that I might be able to get away with talking to my mother "that way" but not to him. He's so close that I can't look at him without going cross-eyed, so I look through him. I can feel little droplets of saliva catapulting onto my face as he screams at me, and that's about the only thing I can focus on in this moment, other than feeling paralyzed with fear.

He seizes me by the arms and tosses me onto my bed, then grabs a couple of pillows and throws them at me forcefully. My mom is in the room at this point, screaming at him to stop and get out. He finally exits the room, slamming the door behind him. My mom goes after him, and I can hear them arguing angrily in the living room.

I'm trembling so badly that it's challenging to walk over to the door, shut it, and lock it again without my knees buckling. I manage to grab a stuffed animal and hide in my closet with a blanket over my head. Now on floor in the dark, I'm scared and sobbing.

"I hate him so much," I whisper to myself through clenched teeth. I feel small. Powerless. Terrified. Humiliated.

Worst of all, I'm convinced he hates me, too.

## THE PROBLEM CHILD WITH THE PROBLEM ATTITUDE

I felt misunderstood as a kid. On one hand, I was sensitive, empathic, and compassionate, feeling people's emotional pain as if it were my own. I genuinely cared about helping others and often made it a point to show kindness to other kids who felt like maybe they didn't belong.

On the other hand, I could also get pretty damn sassy. To parents, teachers and other authoritative figures alike, I was known for talking back and being argumentative. I demanded to know why I must do something I didn't want to do, and "because I said so" was an unacceptable answer. I had a lot of anger festering within, particularly toward the adults in charge who tried to make me feel like I wasn't in control.

By the time I was four years old, my mother had divorced my father and married Rick, who was inclined to use physical intimidation, verbal attack, and shouting as a means of asserting dominance and control in the family. When challenging situations and emotions arose, he was prone to shutting down and putting up walls, turning to alcohol to numb out. He somehow managed to hide his addiction from my mom for a while, but it became apparent soon after they got married. My mom, while loving and well-intentioned, was strong-willed and struggled with debilitating fear and anxiety. She had a "bulldog mentality," as she would call it, and needed to be in control.

All of this proved to be the perfect storm for emotional chaos, making for a very unpredictable home environment. Things could be volatile, if not downright scary, between her and Rick. I've never witnessed any physical violence between them, but their fights escalated quickly and were rife with insults, cussing, and name-calling.

All things considered, my own confrontational nature isn't such a shock as I look back at my youth, yet no one knew how to deal with me at the time. Not only did I have little regard for rules and boundaries, I was also angry, defiant, and manipulative and felt like I had no voice, so I gave myself one at all costs. My childhood diary can confirm that I spent quite a bit of time being punished, and the consequences could be disproportionate to the offense. Usually, I was grounded for a minimum of a week, even up to a month in a few cases. But ongoing punishments clearly weren't solving the problem.

My mom and I constantly butted heads. Even though she was generally the warmer, more affectionate and compassionate parent, we were too alike in our stubbornness. I challenged her authority at every turn, and more often than not, I was much more committed to getting my way than she was to holding steadfast on her limits. This only taught me that if I pushed the boundaries hard enough, I could shift them.

Dealing with Rick was much different. Because he was a totalitarian, there were immediate and sometimes harsh consequences for questioning his authority. I feared him, which naturally made seeking my mom a much more attractive option when permission was required, as she was more likely to bend.

Back then, I didn't fully understand why I treated my mom that way, which felt really confusing. I knew I loved her, and I certainly favored her over my stepdad. But when we got into shouting matches, something else within me took over—maybe something within *both* of us. There were times we *both* ended up in tears during a fight.

"WHY are you like this?" my mom demanded through her sobs. "You used to be such a sweet little girl; we used to get along so well when you were little! Why do you act like this and treat me this way? I don't understand it!"

I didn't want to admit it in those moments, but statements like that ripped me up with guilt and shame over my behavior. Especially because I didn't *want* to be so nasty. I *wanted* to be that sweet little girl who was worthy of her mom's loving affection. But once my anger was activated, it felt like a monster that couldn't be tamed.

The same year that Rick punched those holes in my door, I became so consumed with rage after another fight with my parents that I couldn't contain it. When they were out of sight, I grabbed a steak knife from the kitchen drawer and stabbed the wall repeatedly. I remember thinking to myself how much I hated them—but even more so, how much I hated myself. I also recall staring down at that knife and, for a brief moment, thinking maybe it was better if I wasn't around anymore. I was only ten years old.

My parents, nearing their wits' end, forced me to see a church counselor and even put me in Christian school in hopes that these influences would straighten me out. But these decisions served only to reinforce a feeling that something was wrong with me, that I was a problem child with a problem attitude. I felt like my own parents didn't even like me. And if my parents couldn't like me, how could I possibly like myself?

I lacked the self-awareness and emotional intelligence to articulate that the source of my rage was the lack of love, empathy, respect, and integrity in our household. Even more frustrating was the fact that *there was nothing I could do about it.* No one seemed to care about how I felt; they seemed interested only in correcting my behavior.

I hated it when Rick treated my mom so contemptuously, blaming and openly condescending her. It was easy for me to villainize him because his transgressions were more obvious. But it was also frustrating when it felt like my mom wasn't respecting and standing up for herself or protecting my brother and me from such tyranny. There didn't seem to be any boundaries for when enough was enough. The more he attempted to push her away, the tighter she seemed to cling to him.

I suppose the truth is that I didn't respect either of them, and that much was evidenced through my behavior. But I didn't understand why I was expected to treat them any differently than how they treated themselves or each other.

I believe that my relationship with my biological father was my saving grace. He provided a lot of emotional security and stability that was missing for me at home. I'm grateful that he always remained actively involved in my life as best he could, although it was largely through phone calls and letters. He became a commercial airline pilot after he retired from the U.S. Air Force and lived several hours away, so I got to see him only once every other month, sometimes less often. Our relationship wasn't without its own set of challenges, but he was fun to be with and demonstrated a healthier balance of boundaries, discipline, and love. He always made me feel provided for, taken care of, important and missed.

He knew I had behavioral issues, especially since he typically witnessed them directly for the first day or two of almost every visit. There was almost always an initial battle of wills, yet I straightened out much more quickly around him. After all, my time was always so limited with him, and I craved his love and approval more than anyone else's.

As much as he recognized my attitude problem, he was unaware of how bad things were at home, so he didn't know how to help or what to do but defer to my mom. And she was unaware that the dysfunction in her own marriage was setting the tone for all interactions within our family.

## NO ESCAPE

Shortly after I graduated high school and moved a few hours away to attend college, things back home took a dramatic turn for the worse. Devastated by some major personal losses, Rick's drinking spiraled out of control more than ever before. My mom leaned heavily on me as his behavior became more erratic and malicious. I was constantly getting a barrage of texts from her or spending hours on the phone, listening to their latest drama. I wanted to be empathic because I cared and was concerned for her safety, but sometimes it was too much. There were times I avoided her calls or didn't reply to texts. Every update only re-ignited my rage toward Rick and my frustration with my mom's lack of self-respect.

Here I was, finally getting a fresh start on my own life, and this drama was following me. It wasn't fair. Why were these problems still my problems? It was so stressful that my grades started to slip, and I even dropped some classes to avoid failing.

## ENOUGH IS ENOUGH

All of the drama came to a head shortly after my college gradua-tion. I had plans to move to Texas but didn't have enough money yet. Despite my reservations, I decided to move back home for a few months and work at my parents' upholstery shop as a short-term solution, rationalizing that it was great money and I could live rent-free.

A week before my big move to Texas, I was working my last day at the upholstery shop. I had told Rick in advance that I had a hard stop that day due to my bridesmaid duties in my friend's wedding rehearsal that evening. Before traipsing off to the bar during business hours, he asked me the "favor" of delivering a job to its owner on my way back home because his other two runners were busy. I expressed concerns about my availability since I knew my last job of the day would be time-consuming, but he basically told me to make it work.

As predicted, that last job swallowed the entire afternoon. I was already running 20 minutes late for the wedding rehearsal, so I didn't have time for a last-minute delivery. Stress and frustration welled up as I anticipated his irritation at my failure to come through.

*If this is so important, why isn't he doing it himself instead of going to the bar? He knows I have somewhere to be.*

I called his cell phone before leaving to see if there was another solution, but I got his voicemail. I left him a message, hopped in the car, and sped home. Fifteen minutes later, my cell phone rang. It was him. And boy, did I get a drunken earful.

"You don't care about anyone but yourself. You're really just a selfish bitch. And you know what? You can go fuck yourself!" These were the last words I heard before he hung up on me.

I was so pissed that my heart was pounding and my face was hot. Shaking with fury, I called him back but only got his voicemail.

*Who the hell does he think he is, talking to me like that? He left work early to get loaded, charging me with something that wasn't even my responsibility, knowing I had a hard stop today. But he's gonna try to blame me, name-call, and cuss ME out for his inconvenience? Oh, hell no!*

That was it, I'd had enough. And this time, I could do something about it. I was no longer a captive audience whose life was dictated by the whims of the inebriated and the dysfunctional. I was an adult on the verge of starting a new life hundreds of miles away.

That day, I decided to cut him out of my world for good. That phone conversation ended up being our last for several years.

Even though my mom remained married to Rick for a few more years, I still maintained a relationship with her. It presented certain challenges around my visits back home, but she usually made arrangements so that I could avoid having to see him.

## BREAKING THE CYCLE

As an adult, I found myself in relationships that sometimes alarmingly resembled that of my parents. My first live-in boyfriend sometimes shouted, threw things, and verbally attacked me when he got angry. In one instance, he backed me against a wall and screamed in my face, his nose touching mine as he cussed me out. It was disturbingly familiar. I was suddenly a scared little girl again in the face of a tyrant, cornered and helpless. How had I ended up with a man just like my stepfather?

This provoked intense soul-searching. I realized that my impassioned animosity for my stepfather had served only to poison my own soul. The fact that it was playing out in my relationships was eye-opening. I spent years fantasizing about all the horrible things I'd say to Rick, if I ever saw him again, to make him feel just as small and despised as he had made me feel throughout my life. But my resentment wasn't making any difference to him at all—and why would it? For all I knew, he was happy to have me gone, too. I was the one who had to live with this unresolved rage, still affected by it years after my last contact with him. Even worse was realizing that my inability to let go of my pain meant that I was inadvertently granting him power over me.

Hell, I'd be damned if I was going to give him any opportunity to control me, even indirectly. It stung even harder having to admit that I wasn't just allowing it, I was clinging onto it! I wanted so much better for myself—needed, demanded better! I knew something had to change to get there.

*But what? How? How do I stop suffering?*

Something inside me whispered back: You must forgive.

*Um, excuse me? Ha! No. I'm good, thanks. You're funny . . . . What do you mean, forgive? That's the last thing this guy deserves! I endured way too much shit for way too long, and it's HIS fault. He's not even sorry! Even if he is, he doesn't have the guts to apologize to me. I deserve an apology at LEAST!*

That's when I stopped. Essentially, I had just listened to myself argue that the power over my healing belonged to my transgressor, not to me, because I couldn't heal without his remorse.

I needed to take ownership of my healing, to be the one releasing myself from my pain. The only way I saw that possible was if I learned to change my perception of Rick as a heartless evildoer. Was there any chance there was more to him than that?

I reflected on any possible redeeming qualities and things to be grateful for. He was a street-smart entrepreneur who taught me and my brother responsibility, a good work ethic, and financial independence. We always had a roof over our heads and food on the table, and we usually had even more than we needed. He wanted us to be successful in life and helped in various ways, including providing me a dependable car when I went off to college and setting me up to run my own branch of my parents' upholstery business so that I wouldn't have to rely on minimum-wage jobs to pay for school.

That's when it hit me: all these things were his way of demonstrating of love for us, for me.

Okay, so maybe he wasn't pure evil after all.

I learned from my mother that his own upbringing was burdened with unresolved rage, animosity, and abuse. His environment was also volatile, at times even violent. Though his shitty adult behavior was utterly inexcusable, I saw that it was his way of "acting out," exactly like I had done as a child, unaware of how to manage my emotions. I saw myself in him and could strangely relate for the first time. Emotionally, he was still a child deeply rooted in the dangers of his own formidable childhood, trying to survive the inherent pains of the human experience.

My willingness to view him through the lens of loving compassion was my first step on my journey to healing. I needed to forgive—not because he deserved it, but because *I* deserved it. Because I wanted freedom from the prison of my bitterness in which I'd kept myself locked away all those years.

I had an entire childhood's worth of stories to unravel, so the healing process took years to navigate. Yeah, you don't just wake up one day like Cinderella with birds and mice singing your praises as they adorn you with ribbons. It's excruciating to make direct eye contact with your emotional pain. With each flashback, it took hard work to reframe Rick's actions as cries for help, which forced me to hold space for him. There was something transformative about that, though. My willingness to look without total judgment intrinsically helped me understand that the way he treated me was an unconscious reflection of how he felt toward himself.

This willingness led to an important discovery: As "the problem child with a problem attitude," I had unknowingly developed a belief that I was not good enough, that I needed to change myself to be accepted or worthy of the love I craved. This was evident all throughout my life. I changed myself so readily to fit in with any crowd that "adapts well to new environments" was proudly stated on my resume. I repeatedly chose challenging relationships because I believed that being loved was a privilege that must be earned with hard work. In fact, I completely lost myself in another tumultuous long-term relationship because my own self-worth was dependent upon my partner's validation of me.

That breakup was the most painful I had ever experienced. I had already learned to forgive—now it was time to release the unhealthy beliefs that led me into codependent relationships in the first place. As gut-wrenching as it felt to detach, that experience turned out to be a powerful mentor that permanently changed the course of my life. I learned to love myself and feel worthy of my needs, which wouldn't have been possible at the time had I not already laid the foundation for healing. It was time to own my shit, dig deeper, and discover who I really was outside of my victim narrative.

I scoured the depths of my inner abyss and came face to face with that scared little girl, still hiding in the closet of her bedroom. Still hiding from her authentic self and all its glory. She feared failure, so she aimed low. She never felt good enough, so she settled for mediocrity. She masked her insecurities by criticizing and blaming others. Worst of all, she didn't know how to enjoy her own company. I was finally witnessing her, wholly and honestly, for the first time, and I embraced her with fierce love. If I could grant loving compassion to one of the most infamous antagonists of my past, I sure as hell could grant it to myself, too. And I did.

Only a few years later, I'm now in the healthiest, most rewarding relationship I've ever had. Our partnership is constructive and interdependent, has healthy boundaries, and provides each of us space to be fully accepted and appreciated for who we are. I'm living authentically and speaking my truth, which has empowered me to push beyond the limits of what I believed possible for me. Not only am I awed by the amazing opportunity to share my story here, but I've boldly left my corporate job behind to answer my higher calling: coaching others on how to release themselves from the pain of emotional trauma, so they can fully embody their inner empowered badass.

Take it from me—self-discovery is not for the faint of heart. It's guaranteed to surface some painful shit you thought you had laid to rest, and there will be tears. Lots of them. Facing the darkest, "ugliest" parts of your soul takes some real guts. But if you're brave enough to look inward, into the abyss, perhaps you also have the courage to conquer it.

## APPLYING THE LESSONS

1. Forgiveness is the antidote for unresolved anger. This concept is contrary to human nature (i.e., ego). Life is messy and emotional suffering is inevitable, yet it all serves a purpose. We cannot grow without facing adversity, and overcoming challenges helps us gain confidence by proving to ourselves that we're capable of slaying demons. According to 11th century Tibetan tantric Buddhist yogini Machig Labdrön, "A [demon] is anything that obstructs the achievement of freedom."

2. On a spiritual level, unfiltered egoic beliefs often keep us imprisoned in bitterness and obstruct our path to truth. We must deliberately release unhealthy beliefs to become free. Every great difficulty in our lives is a teacher whose sole purpose is to drive us away from dysfunction and reveal where growth is required. Pain is meant to be only a temporary consequence, not a life sentence. If you don't resolve it, it will poison you.

3. Forgiveness is NOT about the other person, it's about YOU. It has nothing—I repeat, nothing—to do with someone's worthiness to receive it. It's truly an act of self-love which liberates you from the agony of your past. Your negative emotional patterns don't need your consent to keep disrupting your life. They will always remain until you face them and work to heal them. No one needs to (or is going to) grant you permission to mend yourself! You must take ownership of your own healing by consciously choosing to release neg-

ativity.

4.  Emotional freedom requires a willingness to shift your perspective. Ultimately, forgiveness is the willingness to embrace a paradigm shift in exchange for emotional independence and power. However, this freedom isn't free; it requires sacrifice. Sacrifices are symbolic of love and devotion through relinquishing something significant and valuable. And since the ego values things such as the "right" to be angry, blame, and judge, these must be relinquished. Doing so provides you a new map to navigate the terrain of your past (which we do through storytelling), enabling you to assign new meaning and change your narrative from one of victimhood to empowerment.

My path through forgiveness was grueling but transformative! It was crucial for removing blockages from my life, for establishing self-love and self-worth, and embracing a new, empowered identity. As a result, my life took on a much different trajectory. What used to be harrowing stories of the past have been transmuted into power—because I overcame it all. Now, I get to use that experience to help other people with transformations of their own!

# win or lose – it's up to you

**CORINA FRANKIE**

When you're a college freshman who needs $14,000 to pay for school, you get a job. At least, that's what my parents had done. With their example in mind, I called the number on the ad for "Female Car Dealer" in the school newspaper's JOBS section. I thought, surely selling cars would help create the income I needed to stay in school. The woman on the other line, with a thick Russian accent, quickly revealed that the newspaper had misprinted her ad and that it should have read "Female CARD Dealer."

A simple mistake in a school newspaper is the reason my life went from learning about biology, English, and Spanish in college classrooms to developing skills in logic, psychology, and probability theory in underground casino rooms in Texas.

For the next six years, I managed the action at Texas Hold 'em poker tables in all types of venues, from strip clubs to hotel rooms, apartment buildings, and ultimately, my very own cash game. As a poker dealer, I had a great deal of customer service responsibility. I would seat my guests, collect their bets, give them their chips before they started the game, and remind them of the house rules. Part of my role was to monitor the table for signs and gestures of cheating. I'd study the cards for minor damages that players would sometimes make to identify a high card. It was my table. I controlled the flow, excitement, and pace of the game, and, to date, it was one of the most exhilarating learning experiences of my life.

With each hand, I witnessed powerful adult men fall prey to a range of emotions. They were by turns vulnerable, melodramatic, compassionate, eager, bold, disappointed, elated, surprised, annoyed, and fearful. I watched players lose their homes, cars, and families on the poker table, just as I watched some players pull chips that ultimately changed their luck for the better, or at least gave their business another month to meet payroll and put food on the table for their family.

And oh, the stories. When you spend eight to ten hours at a poker table, you hear a story or ten: about the *woulda, shoulda, couldas* of work, marriage, friendship, and family. Through my customers' experience, I began to foster a vision of the type of life experience I wanted for myself. Truth be told, there were some experiences I never wanted to have in my life, while others seemed favorable.

There are nine ways to win a poker hand; after watching thousands of hands, I started to compare the game of poker to life. Through the players' losses and wins, I started to realize that every possible life circumstance is like the cards dealt in a game of poker.

In poker, playing the hand you're dealt is the only option you have. You can't just throw away your hand and start over in the same hand; you use the tools you have at the moment to guide your decisions on how you're going to play. I realized that wishing for a better hand or better luck never got anyone closer to winning.

In my experience, many players ended up losing everything trying to gain it all. Their failure reminded me that if I wanted to get serious about my vision for my life, I'd have to work steadily, using the gifts, knowledge, and tools I currently had. Then one day, I'd have enough tools and knowledge to take home the big win.

· · · · ·

## YOU CAN BE DEALT A GREAT HAND AND STILL END UP LOSING

The combination of my poker-dealing dollars soaring in and an intense, four-hour read of Robert Kiyosaki's *Rich Dad, Poor Dad* ultimately led me to realize that accumulating debt in the form of school loans did not align with my newly-created vision of becoming a business owner and investor. So I made a conscious decision to leave college and instead began to focus my time on making more money and finding a career that would get me out of the rat race.

For the first time in my life, I felt like I had all the answers. It felt as if I had the best hand of them all: the one which would lead me straight to financial freedom, success, and the American dream. I was also confident that the lifestyle would allow me to continue dealing poker late into the night while I took my industry classes, acquired my real estate license, and showed homes during the day.

I went all in toward this vision. I did the work, took the classes, paid the fees, passed the test, and interviewed at all the places.

At the time, I had no idea that my vision of finding my golden ticket to success in real estate would be torn away from me by lousy professionals in the industry I so enthusiastically hoped to become.

I received my license smack-dab in the middle of the global financial crisis of 2007–2008, one of the worst financial crises since the Great Depression in 1930. In the late 2000s, it was easy to find hope in the overall success of the real estate market at large. Realtors and loan officers were increasingly making boatloads of money, and to me, becoming a realtor looked like a career path which would bring me a few steps closer to having it all.

As if going all in on the real estate industry wasn't enough, I had also quit school and slowly phased myself out of working nightly poker gigs. On top of that, I was burglarized. The person who broke into my home stole my identity, as well as all my other worldly assets, even my hamster and the exercise ball he'd run around the house in.

This series of events left me depressed, embarrassed over my choice to quit school, and scared because the rent is due every month regardless of whether life is going well or not.

At my wits' end, I went back to doing what I knew best: dealing cards, in this case four times a week at strip clubs. This worked out well for me because the environment was too loud for chit-chat, and at the time, I had absolutely nothing to say. I was making between $400 and $800 per week, which helped me quickly replenish my savings account.

By this time, my parents were very aware of the choices I had made, which had eventually led me right back to the poker job that got me there. My father, in particular, was not happy I was working in a strip club, and he was very vocal about it; he even made a few surprise visits to make sure I was doing what I said I was doing and nothing more. At the time, the situation felt like it was spiraling out of my control, but in retrospect, I realize now this was the universe's way of setting me up for something else.

· · · · ·

## YOU CAN BE DEALT A BAD HAND AND STILL END UP WINNING

One slow Tuesday night, a good-looking young man walked up to my table and asked me why I was sitting there alone. I chuckled at his question and asked him if he had anything better to do. This young man was Rob Brown, an actor known best for his role in my mom's favorite movie, *Finding Forrester*, as well as in one of my own favorite movies, *Coach Carter*. And yes, he did have something better to do.

Rob ushered me to the VIP room, where I first recognized Joseph Gordon-Levitt, then Channing Tatum, and then Ryan Phillippe—his costars in a movie called *Stop-Loss*, which was being filmed in various locations across central Austin. After a few hours, they were ready to do something else, and because I was the only one with a car, I offered to take them to their next destination.

That otherwise uneventful weeknight was the last time I ever worked a poker table at a strip club. For the next five months,

I chauffeured these young actors around Austin, sharing all kinds of experiences with them. Together, we ran from mobs of adoring women in and out of clubs, playing card games, drinking with the cast and crew, watching comedy, and much more.

After their time in Austin was up, the actors went back home to wherever they had come from, and I rarely heard from them for a few weeks. But a month later, the crew was called back to New York to reshoot a scene. Rob knew from having seen the artwork in my home just how much I wanted to visit New York City, so he invited me up to the Big Apple for the week of the reshoot and offered to host me. I had never been to New York, and I didn't know anyone there, but the opportunity was too good to be true—so of course, I said yes.

When I arrived, Rob picked me up from the airport. He took me to an apartment and said he would be back in an hour to show me around the city. That hour turned into several more, and I began to feel forgotten. I know in my heart that he invited me with a lot of enthusiasm, but I quickly realized on the ground that his priorities were elsewhere.

Eventually, none of that mattered because I'm the star in my own life and I get to decide how I feel about it. I decided to leave the apartment complex to explore on my own. Minutes after I jumped on the first subway going anywhere, I met Mr. Right for the night, an affectionate, hard-working, handsome man who properly showed me the city over the next seven days.

While in New York, I experienced a traditional NYC New Year's. That year's countdown was symbolic for me. I knew in that moment, as we counted down, 10, 9, 8, 7, 6, 5, to the upcoming year, that I would look past the challenges that took place in the first part of that year, choosing instead to see and embrace the amazing opportunities and experiences the second part of the year had brought my way. 4, 3, 2, 1. My life circumstances were simply a thing of the past. On to the next.

· · · · ·

**WILD CARD**

About a year later, two friends convinced me to partner with
them to start an underground poker game in a 5,000-square-foot
condo overlooking Lady Bird Lake in downtown Austin. Rumor
had it that the owner of this condo waited four years to buy five
condos next to one another so that he could gut them from within and create one connected living space. The remodeled unit
was connected by two large luxury dining rooms and a commer-
cial-size kitchen. Every master bedroom came with its own guest
bed, living room, and bathroom. This condo was remarkable and
was later nicknamed "First Base" for the excessive partying we
did there.

My two business partners were business owners outside of
our poker game. Jason, a Carnegie Mellon graduate, was on
the brink of selling his first company for millions of dollars to
gaming giant Zynga, and Todd was selling clean energy in open
energy markets across the country. This was the year I officially
incorporated the company I own today, Brand Besties, originally
called Competitive Creations, LLC.

The poker game was successful, but it never grew into the
hotspot we expected it to be. Looking back on it now, we used the
game as a grownup excuse to live in a $5,000/month bachelor
pad and relive our inner college kid days. And I'm glad we did
because, in many ways, that time felt like the college experience
I never had but always wanted. In the end, both Jason and Todd
found their forever women during our time at First Base.

As for me? I leaned into my unique vibrational frequency. My
vibrant personality and the well-rounded communication skills
I'd learned on the poker table led me to create Brand Besties. I
went "all in" in experiential marketing.

Experiential marketing is a deeper bonding experience between
a consumer and a brand. Brand experiences focus on a two-way
interaction that takes place in real time. You often see this type
of marketing objective at a live event where you're able to live,
breathe, and feel the essence of the brand. I found early on that
my zone-of-genius was aligning brands with premium event staffing (brand ambassadors, promotional models, and hostesses) that
would help increase awareness of their brand through face-to-

face interaction and conversations.

My experience with people at the poker tables made me uniquely qualified to pull together an amazing network of talent, partners, and brands in order to develop unique and ownable solutions for my clients.

Today Brand Besties is much more than a staffing agency. We are a real-time communications platform infusing many of the same skills and lessons for life that I learned while at a poker table.

## APPLYING THE LESSONS

### 1. You are the only creator of your life.

As the house dealer, I watched one too many hands where the table became painfully quiet, and for a long period of time players would stare at one another, trying to catch a blink or breath which indicated fear in the faces of their opponents. What I know now is we weren't training ourselves to catch a glimpse of cowardice or fearfulness in our opponents; we were tuning into the vibration of our opponent's energy.

### 2. To live limitless, become fearless.

The thoughts you're thinking right now dictate what vibration you're in. A person who vibrates fear and negativity will attract into their life other people who vibrate fear and negativity. This, as it turns out, is the way people use one another as a mirror to see themselves. I'm a relatively small build, 5 5 ″Latina woman, yet when I wake up, I wake up as my own version of Wonder Woman, ready with absolute certainty that I'm going to have a kick-ass day. When I look in the mirror, I see a strong, confident, and sexy-AF woman. I get to choose! And so can you.

### 3. Play the hand you're dealt.

Try not to contemplate too long on the things that you cannot change. Each time we go through a life experience, good or bad, the only thing left to do is move onto our next experience. Do you see yourself as a remarkable, strong, amazing creator who has come to this planet with purpose, passion, and love, or do you see yourself as simply mediocre because of that failed project or failed relationship? Every moment after that thought should be a moment spent being grateful that you know what mediocre means to you and a time to start thinking about the person you want to become in relation to the mediocre version of yourself you have now identified.

The way you react or respond or internalize what's taking place in your life will depend on your ability to relate to the version of yourself whom you want to become. Don't focus on what's wrong. Focus on what's right.

### 4. Look for the good in people.

There is good in you, there is good in me, there is good in every single person on this planet if you look for it. By sending out good and positive thoughts to the people you meet, good and positive things will return to you, and when good things come your way, opportunities will begin to emerge. Once opportunities begin to emerge, you get to meet new people, and eventually you create this understanding with the universe that good and positive people bring new opportunities into your life.

Sitting at a poker table, it was easy to see people's sadness, drunkenness, fearfulness, rage, and jealousy. But that energy begins to harden you as a person, and so I worked on identifying other qualities of those same people—traits such as confidence, patience, grit, determination, fairness, kindness, and compassion for others. As cause and effect would have it, I became great at giving compliments. As the world has it, people like compliments.

### 5. If you want to win, you must play.

There is a reaction to every action you take on this planet. Therefore, you need to take action to get results.

With every decision we make, there is going to be some level of risk involved. Depending on our mindset, we can win or lose in any situation. In poker, "playing it safe" means that you play a hand only when having the best hand is in your favor. This style of play, in poker and in life, is not only boring, but it also cuts you off from creating any real opportunities for yourself that could yield you a massive payout or reward.

## 6. Uplevel your skills.

In poker, players who win attribute their winnings to skill. Those lit cannons who lose often blame it on bad luck. Success is not an accident. If you want to win, you have to improve your skills.

# creating space for greatness

## DEBORAH WHITBY

We had been married for just over three years in what I always described as a "fun" marriage. As we walked to go get our mail from the community mailbox up the street, I looked down at my seven-months-pregnant belly and felt a form of grief. My eyes filled with tears and I said, "Everything is going to change." Our walks, our routines, our freedom—everything I had found comfort in, I felt, was about to be taken away by the impending birth of our son. Our life was good. Our marriage was good. Why had I made the conscious choice to do something that I now felt might threaten that? Why had I chosen to disrupt the good thing we had going for the unknowns of parenthood? Why was I doing this to myself . . . again?

· · · · ·

### GOOD ENOUGH

Growing up in a two-parent household as an only child for eight years had its perks. We didn't struggle financially, and I had my parents' undivided attention. They talked openly with me about money and would take me on drives to see the "rich people houses." Even when my father worked for a company back then, he always did side jobs for extra cash. I remember how he would walk into the house fanning himself with a handful of $100-dollar bills. I used to ask how much he had to give to his boss. He would furrow his brow and say, "I am my boss."

## BOSSES MAKE MONEY: NOTED

Needless to say, I developed confidence around numbers and money early on. Before I was in grade school, my dad had me do arithmetic in my head, without using my fingers to count. My grandmother counted money in front of me often and sat me next to her while she used a calculator and notepad to do bookkeeping. And many other situations during my developing years cemented my early belief that I was "good with numbers."

In kindergarten, I won a $1 bill from a class visitor because I was the only student that knew what number equaled half a dozen. In first grade, recognizing my potential and interest, the teacher assigned me extra math homework. So by the time I reached the second grade, I had decided to become a math teacher. By sixth grade, I was competing in timed competitions that required me to solve math problems in my head, with no calculator or scratch paper!

Not much changed after the second grade. I just got better at math, and by the time I got into college, I hadn't experienced anything significant enough to change my career path. I had even started getting professional job experience in financial roles right out of high school. And by grace and with a lot of self-awareness, I managed to get into adulthood free of any life-altering trauma, abuse, or vices. When I graduated from college, I stayed the course and became a high school teacher. I was incredibly blessed. My life was good.

That is, of course, until good wasn't good enough.

Less than two short and fast years into teaching, I started to feel a nagging resistance again. Resistance to what, I wasn't sure, or why. But a learned pattern emerged that I am now able to articulate.

*With the exception of a few, the majority of the people that I had been raised around my whole life had settled for "good enough." And if I had ever talked about ideas or topics outside of that norm, I felt disconnected from them, outside of them, and apart from them.*

So I tried to justify being satisfied with where I was and told myself that things were fine and that I needed to chill out. After all, I was just starting my career, for which I had paid private school tuition. Isn't this exactly what I had wanted? But good wasn't in fact good enough. And the need to amplify our lives cannot always be ignored.

I now know this unsettling, resistant feeling as my soul's call for greatness. She shows up to tell me when I've gotten off track and am not living in alignment with my purpose. She shows up to tell me when I'm not playing big enough. And she shows up to tell me when I've become complacent with good enough. I listen when she calls because if you ignore your soul's voice long enough, it gets quieter and quieter, and harder and harder to hear.

I made the decision to transition out of my career. Soon after, I got pregnant, and I found myself walking to get the mail, realizing everything was going to change again.

• • • • •

## RELEASE THE GOOD. EMBRACE THE GREAT

I was right: after Maddox was born, everything did change. We moved from the house we had built only three years prior. We didn't go for walks in that neighborhood anymore. We lost many of the routines we had created together. And I had left the teaching career I'd wanted since I was seven years old.

But what I didn't know that day as we walked to the mailbox was that my son's birth would be the catalyst for a series of choices I would be faced with. And I didn't know that I would choose to lose it all. I would choose to lose it all in exchange for a life lived outside of my comfort zone. For a life of risk, growth, and never-ending phases of evolution. I didn't know that the birth of my son would birth in me an insatiable need to create change, to do better, to be better, and to create a legacy. And, in order to serve God's higher purpose for my life, I would need to let the walls around me begin to fall. That meant saying *no* to the comfortable yes and being both vulnerable and courageous at the same time. It meant recognizing and releasing the pattern of complacency

I'd seen modeled all around me. I would need to release the good in order to embrace the great.

## OUR ONLY TRUE OBLIGATION IS TO ANSWER THE CALL OF OUR SOUL

I I had to depart from much of what I'd known to answer that call and pursue a path that would enable me to leave my son something greater than myself, something that would outlast me. So I got curious and reached out to the few people in my life who I felt could teach me things I didn't know I didn't know. I slowly started to change my environment. I read books; I tried a different job. I even enrolled in grad school to expand my opportunities in the educational field. I dabbled in not one, not two, but three different business ideas. Finally, I connected to what I truly desired: financial freedom, a legacy, and a way to take care of three of most important men in my life—my husband, my son, and my father. I also connected to what I truly desired to feel: validated, secure, and generous. So I decided to take what my father had created for himself as a plumber by trade and put a viable and scalable business model behind it. I now run a successful plumbing company, with my family at the center.

In the two-plus years since I started it, this business has taught me so much about myself, my family, and my values. I feel that I've evolved more in this short time frame than I have in my entire life up to this point. It's been a rapid and rigorous course in self-development, mindset, and money. In our first 15 months in business, we reached high multi-six figures in revenue, forcing me to learn, adapt, and streamline at a quick pace.

We are now an award-winning and award-nominated company, and I have been named by Thrive Global as one of "99 Limit Breaking Female Founders." I've been interviewed and quoted in numerous publications, and now I get to return to my love of teaching and speak to groups and work with individuals on how to elevate their businesses and finances by making and keeping the money they earn.

But with each new ascension of exposure or amplification of revenue and success comes the enduring prerequisite to once again let go of some good, some of the comfort in what may be working and old ways of thinking, in order to create space for new levels of greatness. It's almost never easy, but it's worth it every single time.

· · · · ·

## APPLYING THE LESSONS

One thing I know is that our willpower is finite. There are only so many times that you can have the sheer tenacity and drive to overcome certain situations. At some point, you may need to change your environment. I love me some pepperoni pizza with an ice cold can of Coke. But, most of the friends in my close circle are either vegan, gluten-free, or are making generally healthy choices in which pizza and Coke have no place. So having health-conscious individuals in my immediate environment has almost forced me to up-level my eating habits and pursue a healthier lifestyle. I am not about to be the only one slamming pizza three times a week while everyone around me is living their best, plant-based life!

Same goes with finances, goals, lifestyle, etc. If your closest friends take round trips on the struggle bus, you fit right in living paycheck to paycheck. But if they all have investment accounts and no debt, it's just a matter of time before you start reevaluating your financial choices for the better.

### 1. Take an audit of greatness.

At different phases of your life and business, be brave enough to do an honest audit of your environment and release what is hindering you getting to your next level of greatness in any given area. If you want to eat better, express your creativity, start or scale your business, or simply make a change in your life, try journaling.

Here's a simple journaling exercise to get you started:

• Make a list of the people you spend most of your free time with, whether that's through texting, networking, going out to eat, etc. Are there aspects of these people's lives or businesses that you aspire to have? These aspects might be the things they do in their free time, their finances, the places they go, their hobbies, the quality of their relationships, their level of business success, etc.

- If yes, what specifically is it they have that you would like more of in your life? Why do you want more of these things in your own life? Write it all down. Take note of whether or not these things are an authentic expression of who you truly, deep down want to be, or what you want to have.

- If the people you spend most of your free time with do not have lives that you aspire to live, ask yourself: who do you know that you can reach out to, network with, or spend time with, that does have the aspects of life or business that you aspire to have? Even if you do not know them personally, you can still follow them and learn from them from afar. (Fact: I literally had one single person on this list when I started this journey, so don't be discouraged.)

- Finally, ask yourself: how can I begin to surround myself with these people more?

Maybe that means eating lunch in your car alone while listening to a podcast or audio book. Maybe it means getting vulnerable and sending someone you kind of know a direct message to ask them out for coffee. Maybe it means you hire a coach or consultant. Or maybe, instead of staying home for another mind-numbing night of Netflix, you go to an event you found out about to meet someone you found on Facebook who you admire, and just get yourself in the same room with people who are doing things that interest you. I've done them all, and while they didn't always lead me down the "right" path, they were always a step in the right direction—*Forward.*

## 2. Start small and trust in your ability to figure it out.

Even if you aren't an entrepreneur, you can think like one by looking out for and identifying possible opportunities in your life and then taking small steps in that direction. A lot of the fear that paralyzes us and prevents us from creating changes is that we think we have to blow up our entire lives or businesses to get there. We think it means we will have to quit our jobs, get a divorce, move to another country, stop talking to all our friends, and never eat another cookie again—all in the same day. That simply isn't true.

There's no elevator to greatness; we are all taking the stairs, one step at a time.

Here are a couple ways to start:

- Make a list of ideas, things, or nudges you feel deep down that could be a step toward the greatness your soul is calling you to.

- Is there a creative outlet you want to try out, a place you want to visit, or a person you want to connect with? If you are a business owner, maybe there's a vertical of your business you've been wanting to explore. Ask yourself: *what is the most cost-effective way I can immerse myself in these things?*

You don't know what could be the "thing" that leads to the next thing until you start entertaining new ideas and opportunities and then acting on them. You will learn a lot about yourself, your business, and what you do and don't want simply by trying. Remember that you are made to express the truth of who you are.

### 3. Begin to detach.

Detach from the meaning you have given things. I had told myself that choosing to leave my career and meander in different opportunities meant that I was confused and inconsistent. In fact, it was just part of my process. Once I detached from that meaning, I was free to move through those experiences with grace and acceptance.

Maybe you believe that pursuing your interests first means you are a "bad mother." Maybe a client didn't buy your program, or no one bought tickets to your event, and you have attached meaning to your abilities or self-worth. Maybe you made poor purchasing decisions and are telling yourself it means you are not good with money. None of these "meanings" is absolutely true 100% of the time. In the grand scheme of things, you are likely a good mother, you are competent in your craft, and you aren't homeless, so clearly you have some general responsibility with your finances.

Not everything that happens has to mean something about you. Maybe you just need better sales training to close enrollment. Maybe you need to work with a financial coach to guide you through some money principles and tactics. If I attached meaning every time things didn't go well or every time I needed to do something, I would never get anywhere, and my confidence would be in a gutter somewhere.

Stop attaching personal meaning to the situations in your life, and see how you begin to glide through circumstances, attaching instead to the lessons and opportunities for growth within each.

## 4. Create space in your life for greatness to make its way in.

Create it both literally and figuratively. God cannot fill what you do not leave empty. Create space with your time, your finances, your mind, and your physical space. How can you expect new and great things to come into your life if you can't even find your other sock in the morning?

Change requires that you have margin in your life. You will need margin in your cash flow, in the time on your calendar, in the clarity of mind to get quiet, envision, and create. It's challenging to meet new people if you've maxed out your free time. It's challenging to grow your company when your hours are consumed in the day-to-day. It's challenging to invest in new experiences if you aren't managing your money well. And most importantly, it's challenging to answer your soul's call to greatness if you are not willing to let go of the good.

*What small thing can you do today to create the space needed to move from good to great in your life?*

# be, do and have anything

## DEBORAH YAGER

Here I am, standing at what could be the beginning of the rest of my life. Could I really handle one more failure? One more rejection? One more person evaluating and judging my intelligence? Maybe I'm not meant for greatness, maybe I am only worth what people will pay for my body…

Here's my chance to prove it to myself—I have come so far, so why do I feel like I am holding on by a thread? Logically, I know I have finally made it to the most difficult day of the NLP Trainer's training and have already achieved a level of excellence that only the best in the field of Neuro-Linguistic Programming could even dream of. I'm highly aware that I've almost made it through the gauntlet of a field that is about pure human performance and excellence, but what the hell am I doing here?! I am an ex-stripper and escort. Now here I am, in a very conservative dress, trying to walk the walk of a successful businesswoman, all the while feeling like Julia Roberts in *Pretty Woman*.

As I'm walking down the hallway toward the final evaluation room for presentation certification, internally I focus in my mind, using what I was taught, thinking positively, and pumping myself up with empowerment while the other voice inside my head is filling me with doubts as the butterflies gnaw at my stomach lining.

And then it happened, oh shit! I have HIM?! Of course, the man with the reputation of being the biggest ballbuster was MY Evaluator! The fate of my fragile ego and self-worth now lies in the hands of this Italian hothead with no tact. Fuck! If I'd thought I had any stroke of luck, it's now out the window!

He looks at me and says, with a pretentious smirk, "You're first, and you have one minute." I look around the room frantically for the podium and realized it is missing.

Double shit!

Then, I remember my training. I throw my notes on the floor, fire my resource anchor, and access the fullest power of this "button of success," which in NLP is a secret technique that connects an individual to personal power and resourcefulness at will so that they can perform well. Time to test its effectiveness!

As I start to speak, my voice is shaky, my knees are quivering, and my eyes are straining as I try to read my notes from the floor. "Screw it!" I say internally. And I let go. I let go of anxiety. I let go of perfection. I let go of expectation. I just let go.

I feel a shift inside, and this is largely due to accessing peripheral vision, another NLP resource used to expand awareness from the inside out. Using this tool allows everything to just click: time stops. All my training, all my practice, all the hours I spent busting my ass for the last 18 days shift into total confidence and congruence in the way I speak. I am grounded yet my words are divinely inspired, I feel like I'm channeling the best version of myself, and I don't even need my notes. Suddenly, I realize, I had it all inside of me. I am in the zone. Before I know it, my presentation is over.

As I stand there, waiting, my heart starts to race again. The "ballbuster" finishes marking his notes, looks at me with a frown, and pauses for what feels like a lifetime. Then he says, "It would be an injustice in the world if you don't go out and train this stuff."

I am shocked at first; I think it's some sick joke. I'm waiting for him to tell me he's totally messing with me and that I've actually failed. Then I realized he's serious. As I sit down, I'm on cloud nine. My shock begins to wane, and my confidence starts to grow deep inside, and I think to myself, "Maybe I can teach NLP after all."

Later that day, as we sat at graduation, I got my next reality check. Our lead trainer congratulated us and sent us forth with this thought: "You can be the best NLP trainer in the world. but if you don't have bums on seats then who are you helping?"

That statement kept ringing in my head as my husband, Brandon, and I made the journey from Las Vegas back home to California. I thought of how far I had come since I was first introduced to NLP. I realized, again, how impactful learning NLP, Time Line Therapy®, and hypnosis had been on my life.

Time Line Therapy® is a method of releasing trauma, negative emotions, and limiting beliefs from the past by accessing your personal internal time line. This method can also be utilized to supercharge your ability to create the future you desire. Hypnosis is a powerful process which allows you to get in touch with your unconscious mind to create massive change and tap into the body's innate intelligence and ability to heal itself.

This work has been a game-changer for me.

· · · · ·

As far back as I can remember, I struggled with anger, fear, and deep-seated unworthiness which created a void inside of me. I remember being in first grade, stuck in a room taking those degrading tests to find out if I had a learning disability.

That diagnosis crushed me. It was all I needed to affirm what I was already feeling: I wasn't good enough or smart enough to ever amount to anything. It was as if I took out a knife, clipped my own wings, and gave up on my ability to fly. Soon after, realizing I now had an excuse for my problems, I started hanging out with the wrong crowd and seeking anything to fill this void and reaffirm my own darkness. Because of this, I was deeply attracted to, even seduced by, the dysfunction of the dark side.

By 13, I was using drugs and alcohol to self-medicate my fear and anxiety and to numb the pain of low self-worth. At 16, I dropped out of high school, started stripping, and soon after began escorting. I loved being high on any drugs I could get my hands on. I thrived on the attention, the power, the control; I loved controlling men, taking their hard-earned money and then discarding them like trash. I loved when these men would tell me how much they loved and wanted me, how beautiful I was, and the false sense of confidence that kept growing—a shell, protecting the little girl who was screaming inside in fear and total disgust of who she thought she was.

Fast forward to 29 years old: I had been in a series of abusive relationships, spent much of my life wasted on alcohol, popping pills, and had just relapsed on meth. Many times, I wanted to do something different, but I held back, believing I wasn't smart enough or worthy enough to do anything else. At a deep karmic level, I felt not only that I was unworthy of a better life but also that I deserved to suffer. And I did, almost killing myself in the process.

. . . . .

After I hit rock bottom for what must have been the fiftieth time, I realized that if I didn't change, I would find myself either in jail or dead. I started to search for something to help me get control over my life. That is when I was introduced to NLP, Time Line Therapy®, hypnosis, and NLP coaching. I began my journey toward the first level of NLP training, my awakening.

One of the processes I learned is called Parts Integration, an extremely powerful modality to resolve internal conflict. Basically, it is a way to accept and unite all the "yous" who live within you. This was groundbreaking for me because I lived with the constant struggle of managing the highs of manic behavior and the lows of falling into deep depression. For the first time in my life, the two people inside of me, the devil and angel, stopped fighting. It was silent inside my head, and I felt whole. It was nothing short of a miracle. That training changed everything. I started to love myself for the first time and believed more was possible.

By the time I attended Master Practitioner training a year later, I had begun to know my worth and to believe that I deserve healthy, loving relationships. That's when I met and fell in love with my now-husband. I had the courage and strength to walk away from my destructive lifestyle and truly start to heal the many years of abusive relationships I had with myself and others.

· · · · ·

On the long drive home after certification, the concept hit me that most of the people in my past were either in jail, dead, or strung out on drugs. I remember thinking, "And yet here I am; look at all I have accomplished, how far I've come. I am a survivor. Not only that, I am thriving!"

I had overcome my fear of public speaking and proved to myself I wasn't illiterate. I wasn't stupid! I could learn to read and write! I had completely transformed myself in a very short period of time and with all the odds stacked against me. I was proof that no matter what you've done or been through in the past, you CAN change.

I had separated myself from people and circumstances that were leading nowhere. I had divorced myself from a life bent on destruction and rebuilt my life with my own mind and my own determination. And I was ready for the opportunities and challenges ahead. Not only that, I felt like everything was possible!

My evaluator was right; it would have been an injustice if I didn't go out and "train this stuff." So many people were suffering just like I had. I thought about his words and about what it would take for us to be great NLP trainers and what it would take to fill seats. I knew that sharing this life-changing work was my soul's purpose, and yet I felt the familiar deep fear, doubt, and unworthiness rush over me. Again.

When we got home, Brandon was all fired up, and he said to me, "Babe, let's do our first training next month, like our trainers said!"

I screamed, "I'm not ready!!" and ran into the house in tears. I felt so defeated. I was so angry and frustrated—with him and myself. He didn't understand. He was confident and naturally good at everything. I asked myself, "Why can't I be more like him? Why am I such a baby? What if someone finds out about my colorful past? Who would want to learn from me anyway since I obviously don't have my shit together?" Once again, I felt unworthy and like I was a fraud.

So, I retreated. I continued to work in an administrative position at Brandon's real estate company. The plan was to gain confidence and prove to myself that I was worthy enough to start leading trainings. Time went by, and I got into a comfort zone, going through the motions. I felt unhappy, unfulfilled, and trapped. I lashed out at Brandon, and our relationship suffered. I was so frustrated with him and with myself; maybe I wasn't meant to be an NLP Trainer. I thought about packing my shit and moving back to Vegas and starting over again. I went so far as running scenarios in my head of sneaking out in the night and calling my old sugar daddy for money so I could go score some drugs to lose weight and go back to stripping and forget everything I learned about NLP.

Through it all, though, I used my NLP tools. I spent hours doing emotional clearing work, uncovering repressed memories from the past and continuing to heal. Despite my efforts, I still felt stuck. Why wasn't I more confident than when I left Trainer's training? I had done the emotional clearing work. Where was the shift I needed in order to feel confident enough, strong enough to move forward and get after my dreams?

· · · · ·

## REACHING OUT FOR HELP

I needed help. What I was doing definitely wasn't working. So I reached out to Laura, a dear friend of mine and fellow coach. She invited me to come back and assist at an upcoming Practitioner training. Yes! I jumped at the opportunity. I needed a reboot and needed to get out of my environment to get some clarity on my life and goals.

During the training, we had a heart to heart. I started to cry. I told her how I felt stuck. I didn't understand why I couldn't move forward, or how, even though I had done so much clearing work,

I still didn't feel confident.

"STOP," Laura said. "You have already cleared it ALLLL. You've got nothing left to clear!! You just gotta get the monkey off your back. You are never going to be ready. And it is never going to be perfect. You just have to do it. Even if it is for only two people, it doesn't matter. Just do it. Action builds confidence."

It never occurred to me that confidence comes from doing. I always assumed that I would feel confident and *then* take action. I realized that a need for perfection was getting in my way. I was spending all my time and energy getting ready to get ready and spinning my wheels. Perfection doesn't exist . . . except in the mind. I was comparing myself to my trainer and others who had been in the business for 35 years or more. Of course, I wouldn't be that polished in the beginning. Besides, I would do it my own unique way anyway.

That realization brought my thoughts full circle. I remembered the words of our trainer at graduation: "You can be the best NLP trainer in the world, but if you don't have bums on seats, then who are you helping?" That statement was made right before the trainers began talking about sales. And sales was something I had run from in the last year while working for the real estate company. The word itself gave me a visceral and negative reaction.

A huge part of what it takes to be a trainer is mastering the ability to sell. Selling programs, selling ideas, beliefs, and the value of personal investment.

I wasn't like Laura, who was and is an amazing saleswoman—one of the best in the field of NLP. "Can you help me sell?" I asked.

Laura smiled and asked, "Deb, what is preventing you from going out and making sales?"

The answers came. I was afraid—afraid of rejection, afraid of looking stupid, afraid of being afraid. I didn't want to look stupid. I also didn't want to bother people, I didn't want to be pushy or "too salesy." And the big one—I was scared to ask people to pay me for my skills and expertise. Yikes!

Laura took on my fears head on. She said, "Deb, it is your responsibility to get out there and sell this stuff. Look how far you have come, and at the role NLP has played in that growth. You have to get out there and share your story. Think of how many women are suffering and how many are stuck in abusive relationships. Think of how many people are stuck in careers that are wrong for them, how much they yearn for something more and don't know how that can be possible. Besides, sales is just like coaching! I want you to go out there and talk to people and pretend that you are simply coaching them. Come in with the mindset of 'How can I help this person today?' Be genuine, care about what is going on in that person's life. Ask questions and identify their goals and life passions. You are just building a relationship and educating that person about what is possible!"

Holy shift! I felt it. My mind broke through the limitations I had created. I understood. I knew what I needed to do and finally, I felt confident enough to take that first big, scary step and get after my dreams.

I did it. And you can too.

· · · · ·

## APPLYING THE LESSONS

### 1. Set a goal.

Always start with the end in mind, and be specific.

For me, it was having four people in my first training. Make sure you are setting your goals big enough. Business experts often suggest that if you are hitting 90 percent or more of your goals, you are not setting them high enough. As I look back on my own journey, I realize I didn't set my goals big enough in the beginning. Now I set them so big that I rarely get within 80 percent.

### 2. Take massive action outside your comfort zone.

Ask yourself, "What is the one thing I can do right now that, when done, will cause everything else to fall into place?"

women entrepreneurs · WE ARE BRAVE

For me, identifying that one thing was simple—what do I need to do to generate leads? The answer was also simple: Talk to people. Everywhere I went, I made a point to introduce myself, spark a conversation, talk to people. Simple, but not easy.

In the beginning, it was super awkward. In the past, I've struggled with social anxiety. It was a challenge to look people in the eye, let alone have a conversation with a stranger. I figured it was time to train myself to be "not me." Sometimes, I had a great conversation, sometimes not so much. I can't control the outcome. I can only show up and continue taking action.

### 3. Learn from your own movie.

Think of your life as a movie. Acknowledge the patterns and learn from them. Failure is feedback. Incorporate the learnings and take more action.

At first, I would take failures and rejections personally and beat myself up for looking stupid or saying the wrong things. Then I recognized and acknowledged that pattern. I asked myself where this pattern began in my life. I used Time Line Therapy® to go back into the past, identify the pattern's root cause, and let it go. The more I value, trust, and love myself, the less I need other people's approval.

Another learning for me was the understanding that every failure is a success. I realized that every time I took action and failed, I actually succeeded in breaking my old pattern of giving up before I even started. So I started taking more action, incorporating the feedback from every conversation, finding the lesson, and getting better each time I tried again. The more I did it, the easier it got.

### 4. Trust yourself and the universe, and take more action.

As I work with my clients, at some point in the coaching process there is the one call I always get: "Why isn't this working? I have done all the exercises. I followed all the steps, and I am taking massive action outside my comfort zone. Where are my results?"

Here is the answer I always give them: "Every *no* brings you one

68

step closer to a *yes*." I like to call this "build-up to break through." Most people will put in the time and effort it takes to reach a goal, and then, right when they are on the brink of breaking through, they quit. The secret is this: Keep going.

It looked like this for me. I called anyone and everyone I'd ever talked to about NLP and asked if they would like to come to our upcoming event. 15 noes and two yeses! "I'll take it!" I thought. The training was bumpy and awkward. The first day of training, four people showed up, and by the end of the day, my worst fear happened. Two didn't come back. The rejection was a tremendous learning that, ironically, allowed me to feel more worthy because I shook it off and we finished the training strong.

The next training we did, we had six people, then eight. Each time we learned something new and broke through to another, stronger level of confidence. Sometimes Brandon and I knocked it out of the park and sometimes we didn't. It didn't matter. Each time, we learned something and incorporated the feedback. We grew in the mastery of our craft. Since then I've worked with thousands of people all over the world in the field of NLP, personal empowerment, and personal growth. My confidence has grown each and every time I've worked with clients. They learn; I learn. They grow; I grow.

### 5. There's always more to learn and grow.

In NLP, one of the Prime Directives of the unconscious mind is to always search for more and more. You're here for a specific purpose. We're all in the School of Life on Planet Earth, and we're transforming that life with every decision and action step we take.

I'm on this journey with you, many experiences and learnings later. Recently, I felt ready for another breakthrough on something I'd been putting off: writing a book. All my life I've felt a burning desire to write a book, yet I never believed that I could. So I let that limiting belief go, and I set a goal to publish a book. Two days later, this collaborative book opportunity fell into my lap. I'm so grateful for the opportunity, and, as I type these words, I can feel myself breaking through to another level of my soul's purpose. I feel freer—more truly me—with every word.

So, the question is *What do you want to create for yourself?* You can be, do, and have anything you put your mind to. And then, guess what? There's even more.

# live your truth or die someone else

## DR. DENISE SIMPSON

I found him dead, his body cold as if he had spent the night in an icebox. But not his bedroom, it was like a sauna—hot and musky. I felt the heat envelop my body as I entered his room. It reminded me of the summer heat waves, sometimes reaching 105 degrees, that I loathed as a child in south Texas.

He was my date for my company's Christmas party that evening. Just a few feet away from his bed lay his suit, on a chair. The suit he had pressed earlier in the week next to black shoes so clean you could see your reflection in them. He had a 6'2" slender build, and I'm sure all eyes would have been on us as we walked through the doors. He was not only my date, but he was also my dad.

Our last conversation was the night before over Church's Fried Chicken at my sister's home. He had this look of ease, of release. He was loose and carefree like when he was drunk, which was often. I even asked him if he was drunk. He said, "No, not tonight." That night he felt different to me. He reminded me of a cork no longer submerged underwater. He had bounced back to the surface of the water with ease and buoyancy, his natural state of being.

This ease was a stark contrast to the stress and tension our family was under, especially my father, who was my mother's primary caretaker. By this time, Dad had cared for Mom for almost ten years through her illness. Ten years prior, at the age of 48, my mom had a sharp cognitive decline. Now, she was 58 years old and suffering from Alzheimer's disease.

Dad's health had slowly worsened as the years went by. He had had Type 1 diabetes since his thirties and never quite seemed to get it under control. My early memories of my father were with a beer in his hand and The Beatles playing in the background. I remember, as a little girl, staying awake waiting for him to get home so that I could let him in the front door so as not to disturb my mom, or perhaps it was to save him from my mother's wrath. Other times I would wake up to the sound of him vomiting in the kitchen sink or sprawled, passed out, on the kitchen floor.

He spent his entire life an alcoholic, drowning his pain with cheap beer and serial affairs. I don't know if he ever loved my mother or even wanted a family. It seemed as though she was a burden to him in good and bad health. I can't help but think he hated himself and his life. Did his obligations to his daughters keep him in an unhappy marriage? Did he drink his life away to numb his suffering of not living his truth? Did he even know he could create a life of happiness and fulfillment? So many un-answered questions. Perhaps he never did live his truth and just died someone else.

## FORGING AHEAD WITHOUT THEM

I left in 1995 shortly after high school graduation to build my career and life. I enrolled at the University of Texas at San Antonio, two hours away from my hometown, and was laser-fo-cused on my education and building a resume no one could ever question. I majored in business and leadership while working part-time to gain management experience. I was so dedicated to my part-time job and such a natural take-charge salesperson that they offered me an assistant manager position at a lotions and potions store in one of the busiest, highest-volume stores in San Antonio. After graduating, I went on to earn more degrees, this time a dual master of arts in human resource development and management. I was deliberate in my educational attainment and went on to explore other leadership opportunities in other industries for many more years.

By 2006 I had created a solid foundation for my career. I was a director for a large medical group in San Antonio and a member of many exclusive associations, and I had built a name for myself. I was happily living on the surface, without any personal attachments to anyone or anything, including my family. I was intentional in creating a life which had no resemblance to theirs, a life far different than what I had known. My career was an escape for me. It allowed me to detach from the reality of my mom's illness and my dad's medical decline. I didn't want to make time, not a single minute, to think about what was happening back home. I tried to forge ahead without them.

Meanwhile, my mom's illness was progressing quickly, and my dad's drunken antics were wreaking havoc on our lives. Even though my sisters were there building their families and careers, I found myself making a life-altering decision to return home. The day had finally come when I had to face the reality of the suffering back there.

Upon returning home, it didn't take me long to find a position at a local community college. I was the director of one of the largest departments with more than 80 faculty and 2,500 students. I was focused on my career and establishing a name for myself in my hometown. As soon as I got settled in, I quickly reverted to my old habits, which had protected me for so long. I recreated the life I had in San Antonio. I was again the picture-perfect highly successful woman with some serious career achievements but no personal fulfillment. I was in multiple relationships, living in a two-story apartment, driving a Mercedes-Benz, and hyper-focused on my career and all the material belongings I could accumulate.

I made excuses not to get emotionally involved in relationships, despite what those men thought. Those relationships were unbalanced, with me holding all the power. I treated my lovers like I did my employees, transactionally: comply, and you'll be rewarded, or don't, and you'll be punished. This was a characteristic I learned by witnessing the power struggle between my parents.

As a child, I witnessed so much pain and suffering inflicted by two very damaged people. Dad would come home drunk, Mom would catch him with another woman, and we would flee in the middle of the night to my grandmother's house. He would take her power, so she would take his daughters away. It was a push and pull of power, never equally distributed.

I believed all relationships, including business and platonic relationships, were to be seized and negotiated. I leveraged my relationships by concealing my intentions, never committing to anyone, and controlling their options.

## HIS SUDDEN DEATH

I was in the depths of shallowness and self-interest. I was looking for more success and external validation, finding ways to fill the gaping hole in my soul. The more intense the situation got with my parents, the more destructive I became. I felt powerless at home but was dominating at work and in my personal relationships. My leadership became malevolent and spiteful. The same went for my intimate relationships; I was finding men who were emotionally unavailable so as not to worry about any attachments. The less I could control my parents' pain, the more control I sought elsewhere. This set the course for the rest of my twenties.

Until the day I found my dad dead in the childhood bedroom I shared with my sister. His death was sudden. Here we were preparing for Mom's death, and all this time, we neglected Dad's care. His death caused such immense pain. It was like a punch to my gut, taking all the air out of my lungs. I was taken down to my knees the day I found him, begging him for forgiveness for how I mistreated him. I asked God to be by his side as he transitioned into the non-physical.

## THE ROAD TO MY RECOVERY

In experiencing the death of one parent and awaiting the imminent demise of the other, I realized I had no control after all, and that neither power nor status was going to fulfill my divine purpose and truth. My dad's death taught me that life was not a guarantee and that I must be intentional in creating a life worth living. He and my mom created their lives by default. They relied on fate to direct their lives.

After his death, I spent the next year immersing myself in my personal spiritual evolution, trying to make sense of his death and my mom's condition. I was in deep sorrow and despair, which manifested into depression, self-loathing, and shame for the life I had created.

The first thing I did was resume my readings of *The Teachings of Abraham* by Jerry and Esther Hicks. I discovered Abraham-Hicks (generally known to the public) when I was 19 years old. I was intrigued by the law of attraction and the idea of self-account-ability and probably misused the teachings early on. I returned to the literature and readings, which unearthed the light within and brought peace to my heart. I studied the teachings from Dr. Wayne Dyer, Marianne Williamson, Louise Hay, Dr. Joe Dispen-za, and so many more. I spent thousands of dollars on spiritual workshops and retreats, study programs, and a grief coach to assist me in my recovery.

The road to recovery was the toughest thing I have ever had to do. Recovering from my own addiction to power and status was necessary to discover what was buried by a childhood of trauma and learned behaviors. Old self-defeating habits tried to re-emerge during this process. My brain didn't want to release the familiarity with the heightened feeling of power and control. It had embossed neural pathways of these behaviors and neurochemistry reinforcing the reward in my body with feelings of control. It became a daily war against myself, but one I was committed to winning.

And one day, after many dark and lonely days went by, I found myself feeling lighter, not so serious, and not so sad. I felt like I was coming to life again. I slowly re-emerged into my natural self. Just like that cork bouncing back to the surface of the water with ease and buoyancy.

I found myself seeking deeper meaningful relationships with

others. I found my leadership improving, taking an empathetic approach to my followers and students. The need for control scared me. Now I was repulsed by it and knew it was not my natural state of being. I also started to date again and loved the innocence of courtship and feeling the return to my feminine energy of intuition and compassion. Time went on, and I was enjoying my life in a newly heightened state of immense love, joy, and alignment with my highest purpose.

In 2010, I met a man who vibrated on the same frequency of love and self-respect as I did. He, too, was looking for an equal, one he could love without any conditions while worshipping the ground she walked on. We were matched on an online dating site that March, and after a month of emailing and talking on the phone, he flew to my hometown to visit me in April. After a passionate yet sweet courtship, he asked me to marry him in June, and we quickly planned our wedding for November. Our families were in shock! They couldn't believe I was marrying a man I had just met a few short months earlier. Even now, nine years later, my love for him grows daily.

I have spent every day since my dad's death studying spirituality, new age, and all things metaphysics. I even went back to continue my studies in leadership to earn a Ph.D. in leadership studies. I wanted to learn the foundational theories and truly grasp the fundamentals of leadership.

Today, I am a life and leadership coach, living my divine truth by helping others recover from their emotional trauma and discover their purpose and highest potential. I have spent more than 20 years in leadership in various industries, but mostly in higher education. I have a thriving coaching practice through which I help people lead their lives and take accountability for all that they have created. I help my clients through conscious insights so they can take inspired action to create a life worth living. And I want to help you do the same.

## APPLYING THE LESSONS

There's no need to wait to transition into the non-physical to resume your natural state of being—one of immense love, joy, and alignment with your highest purpose. The following steps will help you begin your journey of recovering from emotional trauma and help you discover your unique truth to start living a life of alignment with your highest purpose.

## 1. Leverage the contrast (or crisis) in your life.

Let's define "contrast" first so we can establish a basis of under-standing. Contrast is the not-so-pleasant stuff or downright shit that life throws at you. It's a crisis in our lives that brings pain and suffering we humans experience at different levels of inten-sity. Contrast is what you feel when you are going through life merrily, and BAM! you get sideswiped by life.

Now I want you to recall some contrast or crisis you have expe-rienced. If you are going through a crisis right now, this activity may not serve you well. I have found that time and emotional distance from contrast are needed before you can take an intro-spective look at the details of the event. For now, recall a past experience. This shouldn't be too difficult; even if you've been on this Earth only for a day, you can't escape the woes of life. Recall a breakup, divorce, death, or illness you or a loved one has expe-rienced. I want you to answer the following questions:

1.   What was your role in the experience?

2.   How did it impact you?

3.   What could you have done differently, if anything?

4.   What new perspective have you gained from the contrast?

5.   If you were coaching someone through a similar crisis or event, what would you tell them you learned from the expe-rience?

These questions are designed to help you look at the role you played and to give you an opportunity to claim your responsibil-ity. There is nothing more healing than taking accountability for your contribution. This process also allows you to leverage the contrast to help on your journey of recovery.

More importantly, this process allows you to get out of your own head and into someone else's heart. When you are able to assist another in their healing, reciprocity is given in the form of healing energy. The act of helping another heals you in return. Don't let your suffering be in vain; share your experiences and what you learned from them. Consider helping another along their healing journey.

## 2. Incorporate a practice of self-love.

Love is a powerful emotion with immense energy. The power of love can heal old wounds and save lives on the brink of extinction. Discovering self-love and self-compassion are what saved me from myself. This is a love that is not narcissistic, nor is it selfish. It's having enough deep reverence for your total well-being.

Changing from a delusional narcissist to a compassionate spiritual being took a lot of work for me but was definitely worth it in the end. You must find the strength to love yourself to change the destructive behavior or remove yourself from a painful situation. During this process, self-compassion is the driver to self-love. Begin with self-compassion, if you find self-love is too hard. When you do find self-love, incorporate rituals to anchor this new belief.

Here are a few questions to get you started:

1. What does self-love mean to me?

2. How does self-love feel?

3. When I practice self-love, I _____.

4. What rituals will I incorporate today to feel self-love when life treats me unkindly?

## 3. Be open to the continuous discovery of your unique truth.

I have realized through my own experience and working with my clients that we must be open to our own evolution. Life is not static—it's intended to be dynamic and always evolving. Static is what my parents knew all too well; they had a fixed mindset, not open to change. Gone are the days of marrying someone out of obligation, going to a particular university because of your parents' expectations, or having children because society tells us so.

You and I have the right to change our desires and passions when we fall out of alignment with them. Just like with the change in the direction of the wind, I too want to adjust my sails when I'm living inauthentically. You'll know if you are disingenuous when your life doesn't feel right. For example, many of my clients take on work obligations that go against their intuition out of fear of losing their jobs. I also have clients who go on dates with guys who "don't feel right" to avoid looking like a bitch. How many times have you felt out of alignment with someone or something? Far too often, is my guess.

If spirituality is your thing or if developing your personal relationship to God, Source, or Universal Spirit is essential to you, find ways to discover what resonates with you. I have incorporated different practices into my spiritual fold because of the alignment they bring me. All I ask is that you remain open to the variety life has for you and never, ever stop discovering your truth.

It's not too late to create a life you love and deserve. I never imagined that someone so ingrained in her own self-interest could be changed forevermore. If I was able to, so can you. My dad's death altered my view on success and fulfillment, but more importantly, he showed me how to live intensely with meaning and purpose. His death led me down a path of spiritual growth and expansion. Without this experience, I would not have unearthed my divine truth, one in which I get to create a life filled with immense love, joy, and alignment with my highest purpose.

# following your north star

## DIANA KUNDROTAITE

The elevator doors opened, and I made an entrance to my office. It was a warehouse-like space, gloomy, with no windows or daylight, furnished with box-like cubicles. The panic, hopelessness, and confusion overtook me. I tried taking deep breaths to calm myself down, but warm, stiff office air made me feel suffocated, my heartbeat rose, and my palms began to sweat.

"Is this really my dream?" I asked myself. I had worked so hard to get here. Working with the United Nations in Canada had been a dream and ambition of mine for years; yet my dream had turned into my own personal prison. I felt small and insignificant, as if I were just another office ant making an appearance in something that falsely looked to be a dazzling life. Landing this position was supposed to be a highlight of my career and secure my place to shine, yet I felt trapped and defeated.

I felt panicked, even though this office was supposed to be my comfort zone, my safe place. That day, I started to feel like something was very wrong. I stepped outside for a moment of fresh air and, instead of returning to what I had thought was my dream job, I never walked back inside. Two months later, I moved to the USA.

• • • • •

As humans, we run on emotion and belief systems, just like cars run on gas. There's no guidebook provided to show us how to play this game called Life. Thus, we forget that we actually are the creators of it. Unconscious emotions and patterns run our lives on autopilot. They dictate and determine what we consciously create in our reality.

My underlying traits have always been ambition and determination. Unconsciously, I associated happiness with success. In order to achieve success, I believed I had to be perfect, smart, strong, and beautiful, and I never questioned where those beliefs came from. All I knew was that my identity depended on these beliefs, so I built my life based on them.

I graduated with a psychology degree, then a master's degree. I worked for the United Nations and lived in seven countries. But I wasn't happy; I felt unfulfilled and disconnected from my true self. My life was filled with goals, which in the end felt meaningless. Yet there was still a fire burning inside me, which eventually led me to find my true passion as a clinical psychologist working with women who suffer from eating disorders.

· · · · ·

I have always searched for the purpose and meaning of life. Along the way, I forgot that we ourselves give the meaning to life. We have the capacity to create anything in our lives, but it all depends on the mental perspective and stories we assign to life along the way. Life is like an empty canvas we get to paint with different experiences and color with different emotions. It's a gift meant to be lived. How would you live if failures did not exist, if there were no lessons to be learned, or anything to be proven or improved?

I was always afraid of failure. And thus, by trying to avoid failure, I ultimately avoided life itself. Without knowing it at the time, I was void of a life filled with authenticity, self-expression, and joy. Without my knowing, my search for purpose and meaning was being diluted and determined by unconscious influences that were keeping me from being my real, authentic self. The search and need to express my inner creator was being unconsciously hidden by my fear, doubt, and responsibility.

I actually remember the moment that I started doubting myself and believing that "being responsible" trumps becoming who I am truly meant to become. "What do I want to be when I grow up?" I asked myself as I sat in a classroom surrounded by my fellow 15-year-olds. At the time, I wanted to become "something big" and grow into my fullest potential. A feeling of excitement ran through my body. I felt powerful and curious about what was yet to come.

Suddenly, a crushing, thick, penetratingly cold female voice snapped me out of daydreaming. "If you want to be something, you have to work hard," the teacher said. And just like that, her words became my daily mantra, a motivational force for the next decade of my life The feeling of excitement that I'd felt before became replaced with fear, duty, and a need to perform. And so I did. I worked hard. One goal followed another. The to-do list never ended, but at least I was checking off all the duty, hard work, and responsibility along the way.

As I achieved my goals, I felt amazing; however, the happiness, ecstasy and gratification were short lived. With every new goal I reached, the satisfaction became shorter and shorter, the feeling of ecstasy continued to diminish, and eventually having achieved the goal was just not enough anymore. In my mind, I believed that something amazing would happen or change once I accomplished the next one goal, yet as soon as I reached that goal, I did not experience the anticipated glory that I expected. Instead, I started to have this strange realization that who I thought I was going to become was who I already was.

· · · · ·

The day I received an offer from the UN was one of the happiest days of my life. But a few months later, the dream turned into a prison. Quite literally. When I look back, the headquarters of the UN perfectly summed up the representation of my dreams. Appealing from the outside, yet so dreadful in reality. A beautiful building with so much promise, yet dull and dreary inside, with an oppressively boring existence, lacking brightness for the future.

The pursuit of my previous dreams of becoming "something

big" now felt wrong, misleading, and dissatisfying, like a promised land where the grass seems greener on the other side. The day I decided to leave my job is the day my definition of success changed its meaning. I realized that the motivation and intention behind everything I do matters. It was becoming the backbone of my existence.

After moving to the United States, I was desperate to change my life. Yet I found myself battling and falling back into my old patterns and behaviors. I desperately wanted to become successful. I had so much potential and many options, but I still had to realize that many of those options would only lead me back to feeling like I was in another prison. Once I truly realized this, I stopped applying for anymore consulting jobs, and I started investing in finding my passion.

This decision began my journey to rebuild and re-edify myself. I began to search for a career that would feel truly authentic to me, and I committed to my life to figuring out my true calling.

To begin, I asked myself, "Where did my previous need for success come from?" This one simple question led me to revisit deep-rooted memories of my teenage and young adult years, which I had buried deeply in my subconscious. I refused to acknowledge that phase for years, but it was nevertheless present in directing and determining the course that I had previously taken in my life.

· · · · ·

After deciding to take a break from searching for a job as a consultant, I invested time in my own self-development, and I found myself on a retreat in Hawaii. There I met like-minded people who were refusing to live by their old standards or to remain in a place that didn't serve their true calling. I met a young man who, through his love of his daughter, overcame a heroin addiction and became a doctor at the age of 37. I met a mother who built a six-figure business while being pregnant and homeless. I met a young man who came to the island only to chase the summer and island waves but years later became a pilot who uses his career to continue to chase the summer and island waves.

Yet there I was, still searching for what my story was yet to become.

One evening on the island, a blissful dinner conversation turned into a turmoil of long-forgotten emotions and triggers. Memories from the past flashed through me like movie scenes, and the emotions made my body feel like it had been set on fire.

The memories turned into images from a moment many years ago: My toes were cold, my knees were sore, and I was kneeling on a cold bathroom floor. I gasped for air and purposefully avoided the pain in my stomach and the tenderness in my throat. My whole body felt weak, and every movement made my head spin. I felt like I was about to pass out.

There I was again, deliberately making myself purge again. Only one bite of an apple took me down the rabbit hole. That day I had made a promise that I would fast. I hadn't eaten properly the day before, or the day before that. It must have been weeks of me avoiding food. I was weak and exhausted. "Just one bite," I promised myself. But one bite of that apple turned into a binge episode, during which I consumed extreme amounts of anything I could put my hands on.

The memory I was having brought me straight back into a phase in my life when I had a heavy eating disorder. At the time, binging and purging were actually my way of trying to win at my life, with no realization that I was actually tearing my life apart. I was terrified of food and what it was doing to me. I was terrified of what I looked like, as my self-concept was heavily measured by my weight. I had severe self-hate and body dysmorphia. Deep down, I knew that life could be a wonderful adventure and the world a beautiful place. But to experience that wondrous place, joy, and miracles, I first had to achieve perfection. This desire for perfection manifested in my life as an eating disorder.

Even though I had this vivid memory while in Hawaii, I actually don't remember many other details of what happened during most binge episodes. Time would stop, and then I would feel complete bliss. Binging made all the emotions and pain go away. It was a way to escape reality. Shortly after the binge, extreme feelings of guilt and shame would drag me back out of the state of blissfulness. The only way to get rid of guilt was to purge. At the time, purging felt like a perfect solution to undo what I had done and to punish myself for my lack of discipline.

My eating disorder started with me cutting back on certain foods and then progressed to my eating only every other day and then to not eating at all. Eventually, it led to unstoppable binging, which eventually led to purging as well. I felt alone and lost. I was in a dark place, in a world where I had no control.

My emotions and negative self-perception started to take over my entire outlook, and this became my reality for many years. The need to become perfect turned into binging, purging, and hiding. In reality, all I needed was to be seen, encouraged, loved, and accepted.

· · · · ·

I adopted a dysfunctional self-perception early in life. My mother, my aunt, and my grandmother all dieted and paid excessive amounts of attention to their looks. Beauty was the thing that was always acknowledged. Beautiful people were complimented, seen, and validated. I felt that, to get attention and validation, and for my potential to unfold, being authentic was not enough. I had to be beautiful.

I know now that feelings and emotions give us valuable information and feedback about ourselves and perceptions of our environment. Not being able to deal with, acknowledge, and appreciate our feelings means we are misjudging important signals about what our true needs and wants are. When our needs and wants are not being fulfilled, deep feelings of grief, anger, and abandonment take place. As a consequence, dysfunctional behaviors and negative self-perceptions develop.

Yet as a teenager and young adult, I didn't know how to express my needs in a way that they would be met. I wasn't capable of verbalizing them and didn't know how to deal with my emotions. Thus, both my internal and external worlds became a fuzzy and unsafe place to exist. Consequently, I thought that my only way to be loved was to be beautiful.

· · · · ·

After I healed from my eating disorder, I dedicated my life to helping other people do the same. Through studying psychology and consciousness, I have realized that everything that happens in someone's external reality is a reflection of what's happening in their inner world. We can choose how we want to perceive ourselves and everything around us. The Ego, which is our identity, self-perception, and preservation, determines how we see ourselves and how we relate to external events, situations, and people. Ego is our experience, based on our emotional stories we tell ourselves, as seen through others' eyes. Ego is very fragile. When someone touches it or looks at it in a way that feels wrong to us, it falls apart, as does our own sense of identity and self-esteem. Our inner world is greatly affected by what stories our Ego tells us.

Humans are here to experience. Our experiences depend on what stories we choose. In a certain way, the Ego is not real; it is an illusion. Yet we identify with it. It becomes real when we choose a story of what happened based on our emotions. If we do not constantly check in with our Ego, it tends to stay fixed in one way of thinking. We must work to reconstruct it and adapt in accordance to a more consciously chosen reality, one that we wish to experience. Ego has the ability to function as a buffer between external circumstances and the stories we assign to it. Our experience is based on our choice of how to experience reality.

Finding my true calling and the success that has come with it has brought me fulfillment, joy, and a sense of meaning in my life; I chose that. I was able to achieve it by reconstructing and adapting my Ego. I have created my self-perception based on how I choose to experience and express myself, without anyone's input. With my new identity, I define myself—both how I see myself and how I see other people. My success and self-love are inner games at which I have learned to excel.

· · · · ·

All of the experiences that come into our reality are meant to be gone through and released, not carried through life. We humans tend to take all accumulated issues and self-damaging beliefs from previous experiences and carry them into new ones. Sometimes an experience is meant to create a duality so that you can have a desire or a wish to experience its opposite. An abused child wishes to know unconditional love. She can do so in her adult life, but only by working through and dropping all the traumatic baggage which she has accumulated through her abusive childhood.

For me, a combination of self-hate and an intense need for achievements resulted in a career with no passion or meaning. That combination has been replaced by the opposite: self-love, excitement, joy, and meaningfulness. At any given moment, we can choose to release all the trauma, dysfunctional behaviors, and negative beliefs that no longer serve us and allow a new, more positive story to present itself to us.

In conclusion, we can play any game or tell any story we wish to in our lives. All you need is a desire and, with trust and allowing, you can create any reality you wish. The universe works in mysterious ways. Life is a great playground, and we should take advantage of it.

# prescribe your own path

## KARLA RODRIGUEZ

"You need to get back to the clinic as soon as you can!" Her voice sounded rushed and worried. I didn't understand what the worry was about—I'd just gotten some blood work to check on my anemia. I had spoken to her this morning, and she told me my anemia was gone. So, what was the deal now?!

A few hours later, feeling annoyed and like I was wasting my time, I found myself driving back in my mom's maroon 1997 Pathfinder, which I'd borrowed for school, to see her at the clinic. Being 17, and thinking this world should treat me right, I didn't know what to expect. Was she wrong for calling me back? I mean, she thought it was important enough to see me in between her other appointments. "She must have had too many people
to keep up with and did not know who she was talking to,"
I thought.

Every time I had an appointment with my doctor, or if I went with my mom to an appointment there, the office was busy. You could set an appointment for 8:00 a.m. and not be seen by a nurse until 8:45 or 9:00 a.m. My doctor must have been so busy that she mixed up some of the files with patient information. This is what I kept thinking, the whole drive there. I kept trying to come up with any excuse as to why she really called me.

I finally got to see her.

This young, thin, female doctor with light caramel-colored skin and brown hair to her shoulders, who I thought was really smart and cool, told me, "Your platelets are too low, and I will need you to take some medicine right away, or I will have to send you to the hospital!" She started explaining something about a hematologist, and I felt like her voice just started to fade slowly . . . . I just stared at her and found myself escaping to another world.

I told her I could not afford to go to the hospital so she should just give me the meds. Turns out, I was diagnosed with idiopathic thrombocytopenic purpura (ITP). It is a disease that makes my body attack my platelets. All my hematologist has been able to tell me is that I probably got sick at some point, and since our bodies make antibodies for viruses they encounter, this specific virus most likely looked a lot like my own platelets.

WHAT?!

It was my first semester of senior year, the year when I was supposed to be celebrating the end of high school and then going to college or the military. The year when my braces were finally taken off for the first time (I have them again)! I was not supposed to be worrying about my body attacking me. I was not supposed to be worrying about getting hit or about driving cars because I could get hurt. ITP can cause excessive bleeding; even minor injuries could be dangerous. It was supposed to be the last year of high school, with the perfect ending and transition to adulthood. Nope. An important step in growing up was to get some news like this.

In December of that year, my general doctor called me and told me my platelet count had gone up but that I needed to keep taking the steroids that were prescribed to me. The second semester of senior year started, and I went on about my days. I took the medicine. I went to get poked even more to check my platelet levels. I graduated from high school on June 4th, 2009, and I kept doing everything normally. Even the steroids became a normal part of my life. Randomly getting angry at my mom became normal. Even waking up at 1 or 2 a.m. to eat something because I was hungry all the time, became a normal thing.

Remembering this makes me feel bad for my naïve, teenage self. Today, rf I am hurting somewhere =, or if I get a cough, I refuse to take any pills.

I am not saying I am against Western medicine. Not at all. I believe it can be helpful if it is really required, but not for the long run. I want my body to learn and adjust itself to what it needs for it to get better.

## MY BODY DOES WORK! SOMETIMES . . .

I was never an athlete during high school or college. In June 2011, my sophomore year at Texas State, I met Jose, who became my best friend, my roommate, and now my fiancé. I had spoken to him about wanting to turn my life and health around. Because of him, I started to run a little and changed my diet. And about three years ago now, my cousin Henry took me to try this thing called CrossFit. He said that since I was already losing weight, I should be okay with this new sport. At the end of that hour, I said, "That's the last time I'll do that!" because it felt like my soul had left my body. I was sore for days and could not believe people wanted to be tested physically like that!

Thirteen months later, I saw a Groupon ad for three months of unlimited CrossFit classes, and for some reason, something inside me said: "Do it." I told Jose we should go try it. I was bitten by the bug. I joined this CrossFit Box and went almost every day for three straight months!

I fell in love with the sport. I fell in love with what my body could do, and I had woken something inside me I never knew I had. I felt fit and stronger than ever. I was already improving my nutrition to try to keep my platelets at a good level so that my hematologist would not have to suggest surgery.

A year passed of my doing CrossFit, and one day it happened— the last thing I ever expected in my life. The last thing I ever thought I would have to worry about.

One night, after falling asleep next to Jose, I was awakened with my mom by my left side. I'll never forget that moment: her eyes trying to get my eyes' attention, stroking my hair, asking Jose to put some alcohol on a small cloth to put on my forehead. At that moment, I did not realize I had clothes on. All I heard her say was "Mama . . . ." This is something Hispanics say to be sweet. Then I heard her praying, thanking God that I was coming to.

What just happened?

Then I heard, "You just had a seizure."

I don't think I processed those words at that moment. Mom and Jose asked me if I was okay. I think I said yes.

I felt numb. I wasn't sure at the time if it was because I couldn't believe what they were telling me, or because my mouth felt swollen from biting itself. I just knew I didn't have a clue what just happened.

Jose told me to go back to sleep, and my mom went back to her room, really worried, of course. She was having to accept the fact that I could sleep after I had just had a seizure. Again, it felt like I was being told my autoimmune diagnosis one more time. I didn't really have any kind of reaction. I did not feel scared. I did not feel like I needed to address this issue right away. I did not feel like I needed to make a big deal out of this one. I was literally asleep and then had been woken up. Without wanting to be woken up—it just happened. This was not my choice.

My body kept trying to fight me. The military decided for me that I could not join. My family started making choices for me that made me feel like I was a victim or someone weak.

One time, at the age of seven, while playing with my neighbors, I fell off a fence onto a brick. I was an average kid, a tomboy, so getting hurt was a normal thing and something I thought was cool. I tried to tough this one out, but I ended up crying to my mother. She yelled with such worry and disgust and asked what had happened to me. Then she looked at my right ankle and saw the blood. She almost passed out, since she has never liked to see blood. As a typical Hispanic mother, she got hydrogen peroxide, Neosporin, and a Band-Aid. I was supposed to be okay after that. Period. I was cured.

On many days while I was in elementary school, I suffered from migraines. I would have to stay seated on a bench because I was not in the mood to play. On other days, I did just fine. Once I got into middle school, I did not feel any weird symptoms and became a normal healthy kid.

My mom tells me that as an toddler, I was so hyper and wild that I was always jumping in the crib, and one day I fell out of it. She said I probably hit my head, and I started having seizures. The doctors had me hooked up to a monitor to check on those seizures, and I was there for a few days. She tries to make this story funny to keep me from feeling fear. The ending to the story is that on one of my last days at the hospital, my dad was in the room with me and stepped out for a minute to get a Coke from the vending machine. He then heard the doctors and nurses running into my room because I had fallen off the bed from jumping. Somehow, a few days later, I stopped having seizures.

The doctors told my mother that she would receive money to help raise me with whatever was wrong with me. In my infancy, my disease was not too common, so they probably didn't even know what to do with me except to give my mom money.

My mom refused to take paychecks from the government for my health, and she strongly believed I would be okay. She changed my diet and helped me get better. Eventually, as a growing girl, I just wanted to eat anything and everything, and my mom was not a mom to look into more healthy options.

## THIS WILL NOT BEAT ME!

March 2016. It was 2 or 3 in the morning. Jose woke me up. AGAIN. I did not know what was happening, again. I was being woken up against my will! My body decided to attack! I looked up at him and my mother, who had those same expressions on their faces. Their eyes were just sad, and I felt guilty. I felt tired. I felt frustrated. This time . . . I felt like crying. I went back to sleep. I did not even listen to a word they said. Or if I did, I don't remember any of it.

The next morning, I made an appointment with my nurse practitioner and was seen two days after my second seizure. The nurse practitioner referred me to a neurologist. I was to see him the very next day. Everything was going so fast. I had to explain to my supervisor why I needed to be late to work. People were going to try to see me as a victim again. That is what I did not want! I did not want this to come out into the world. I just wanted to hide.

The neurologist explained that he wanted me to get x-rays and an MRI. I had to take off work and make up hours to get the tests. Did they even know that I was going to have to pay money I did not have? Against my will, I had to sacrifice things just so somebody could give me a diagnosis I did not want to hear. Jose drove me to my appointments. He also had to take time out of his day at work to drive this "sickly" person around. At least, that is how I felt at the time.

The neurologist brought me into his office and asked "Did you go to school? You went to college?" He looked stunned. I gave him a questioning look, asking why this surprised him. "You have a genetic disease called tuberous sclerosis complex." He explained to me that this genetic disease causes tumors to form in the major organs. Luckily, I do not have them in my bones, kidneys, or any place observed in the x-rays. "You have the tumors in your brain," he explained, "and this is why I asked if you went to school."

## MY BRAIN

On a week when Jose left for a bear hunt in Idaho, I was told that my brain activity was going to get recorded. A nurse came to my house, and we set up two cameras, one at my desk out in the hall where I was going to be working all day, and one in front of my bed to monitor my sleep. I had what felt like 50 connections on my head, and they started to hurt by the third day. This was a week-long observation. I would wake up at 6:00 a.m. since I was able to work remotely, and even with a headache, I had to get work done. The day finally came when the nurse came back to my house to remove all the cables from my head.

I had not washed my hair in a whole week! I had a fanny-pack-looking thing on my waist with the actual monitor system, which kept the records of each day. I was going to finally be able to wash my hair, but I had to be patient for the nurse to take the monitor off. As she took off each individual cable connection, my head felt lighter and lighter. The glue that held the connections on my head was hard as a rock! It literally took three days to really feel like it was all off. It was as if the glue had turned into cement. I had to put up with the residue even after those three days, and I just felt dirty.

The follow-up with my neurologist arrived, and he was surprised I had not had another seizure. He prescribed some medication for me, which I never picked up. I prescribed myself with no medicine.

I made the decision that I was not going to let anyone tell me what medicine I need to take. I was not going to let anyone make me feel like a victim anymore. I decided I would keep pursuing CrossFit and showing my family, friends, and the world that I can listen to my body and that the journey I was on did not have to stop. I was going to fight this shit as best as I could!

Growing up, I learned from my mother that all situations can be turned into something positive. She has always been the person to choose what she wants and how she wants it. Yes, like most people, there have been times when I think she could have been smarter about her choices and the people around her, but she has always been a strong person and has been someone I have always been really proud to talk about.

I have made many choices for myself because of what I learned from her. Over the past five years, I have become a doula, a healthier person, an entrepreneur, and even an up-and-coming writer!

Becoming a doula has been such a gift. I have been able to assist with 23 births! Two of those births were Cesarean births, and all have been huge blessings in my life. I have been able to assist my family and friends to make the choices for themselves, no matter what everybody in the world tells them.

Becoming healthier has made me an example to others that it is possible. Making a choice to live longer and stronger is something I strive for. To live as long as my great-grandmother, who was 100 years old!

Becoming an entrepreneur is basically me making a choice for my future. To be here in the moment, knowing that doing things for me will impact those around me. Becoming a writer was a dream that is now coming true.

All of these are different paths, but they all point to my one true path to keep moving forward and realizing that all is possible. Just make that first step into choosing for you.

To have to think about my autoimmune disease and my genetic disease is hard, to the point where I wonder what I did to deserve this. Then I try to remember I don't have to think about them all the time.

I want to be able to share the illnesses I have with people and not show fear. I want to be able to show you that you can wake up the next morning knowing you get to live another day, and what you should think about is what you will accomplish next.

## APPLYING THE LESSONS

### 1. Make a small goal for the day and a big one for the month.

This could be something as small as eating a banana every day or drinking 10 cups of water per day. Or this could be something big for the month, such as saving a little extra money for another goal you may want to reach. For example, I started saving a little money for my long-term goal of backpacking through Europe one day. All it takes a little time and patience.

### 2. Think about how you can help someone else by sharing what you've got. There will always be someone wanting to learn from you.

So . . . Wake Up. Get Up. Make a Goal. Move Forward.

Buddha is said to have observed that "no one saves us but ourselves. No one can and no one may. We ourselves must walk to path." This is an idea that I live by, and I invite you to do the same.

# my backward journey to inner beauty

## LITA VALLIS

I couldn't sleep. It was the night before my scheduled breast implant surgery. I was going to let a plastic surgeon cut open my perfectly healthy B-cup chest and put in silicone implants to make me a D-cup. It seemed like a good idea at the time. It seemed fun and exciting to imagine how sexy I would look in my clothes with a "more proportionate chest" for my size 10 body. It seemed like a great idea. I had curves and thought this would help even them out, from top to bottom.

So why couldn't I sleep?

The choice made perfect sense when I talked to the women who worked at the office and who had done the same thing and loved the results. I read the brochure in the plastic surgeon's office, and it all sounded so wonderful and easy and empowering. It made sense.

So why couldn't I sleep? I looked at the clock over and over again . . . 2 a.m. . . . 3 a.m. . . . 5 a.m. . . . why couldn't I sleep?

Thoughts raced through my mind. What was I doing? Did I really want to do it? Do things often go wrong? What is the worst thing that could happen? My husband was sleeping peacefully next to me. Didn't he sense my anguish? Wasn't he worried about me going under the knife? No, he was asleep and miles away. This was my journey, and it was just beginning.

. . . . .

I never had any major self-esteem issues growing up. I was the youngest of three girls, and we all dealt with the normal ups and downs of growing up female in America. Exposure to TV, media, and magazines planted the usual seeds, emphasizing the importance of beauty for a young girl and for all women. My sisters and I would spend hours in the bathroom performing skincare rituals, practicing hair and makeup techniques, playing up our strengths, and lamenting our flaws, but it all felt very normal. It was just part of growing up female.

I dated a little in my junior and senior years of high school. It wasn't until college that dating and boys became a major part of my life. I joined a sorority, so my social life was built into my calendar every week and usually included scheduled social events with fraternities. It was easy to get male attention, and I was embracing this new aspect of myself.

I had a healthy body image for the most part. I was never thin, but I was height-weight proportionate. But I had a break in my healthy body image reality when a boy I was dating told me that my size was why he was breaking up with me: "It's your weight." OH. I see. I should be thinner. I was not enough as a fun, healthy, intelligent, witty, sensitive, caring, young woman with her whole future ahead of her. I also needed to be thin.

That was the conclusion that stayed with me throughout my twenties and thirties. I was never fat; I just wasn't thin. I learned much later in my life that my size was actually in the average range for a woman in America at the time. I wish I had known that then and that I had told him that (among other things), but of course, hindsight is 20/20.

I dated plenty and never had any other complaints about my size or my curves. I met my husband at 34. He loved all of me and my size 10 body. He never made me feel anything less than beautiful. Yet I had a nagging voice telling me I could be more, should be more, or rather less, in this case. Since I wasn't thin, I thought—maybe I should go the other direction and add some more curves to balance out my healthy size 10 frame?

I asked my husband what he thought about me getting a boob job one day after I saw him noticing a particularly busty server at the restaurant where we were having lunch. It wasn't a serious conversation, I was just inquiring, but I could see and feel his enthusiasm shining through his polite response: "If that is something you want to do, I would totally support you."

I started my research.

I selected a plastic surgeon based on a friend's recommendation. We discussed the size and look I was going for in his office, and he was confident he could help me accomplish my goals to even out my fuller look on top and bottom. We scheduled the surgery for two weeks later.

The alarm went off the morning of my surgery after the restless night. My husband rose without concern. I told him about my rough night, and he assured me everything would be fine. He drove me to the surgery center and waited in the room with me. We chatted as the doctor came in to do his final assessment and mark my body with what looked like a black Sharpie marker. He was so casual about it. I could tell this was something he had done literally hundreds of times, marking a body like a chart.

He confirmed that the plan was to put in silicone gel implants with an areolar incision. This would ensure minimal visible scarring. In came the anesthesiologist to drug me up for the procedure. Off I went to a deep slumber, to awaken to my new body and my new lease on life with my size D proportionate tatas out in front to lead the way.

I awoke in the recovery room a few hours later, taped and wrapped up so tightly I could not visibly notice any difference in my chest yet. I was instructed to wear a tight sports bra for a couple weeks as everything healed up, which kept my chest high and tight to my body. I was prescribed several painkillers, which I enjoyed for 10 days until the prescription ran out, and then I was left with Advil to ease my pain. Overall, it was a drama-free recovery.

· · · · ·

Within a month, I was ready to show off my new "girls." My husband bought me some sexy tops and dresses to do just that. He enjoyed my new look, and I enjoyed it, too. I enjoyed it so much for the next six months that I ignored the warning signs my body was sending me, letting me know it was not enjoying these new intruders as much as my husband I and were enjoying them.

Some sharp, shooting pain was the worst symptom at first. The nerve endings in and around my areola were constantly triggered to the point that my husband was not allowed to touch them. This was an unexpected side effect, the opposite of our desired response, but we both assumed it would pass with time.

I had a few checkups with the doctor post-surgery. He assured me that all these issues were totally normal and would heal and pass with time. I wanted to believe him, so I did.

Six months later, I was still having challenges with my nerve endings, and I started noticing soreness in my muscles and joints that I had never experienced before. An achy feeling throughout my body was becoming a new normal part of my daily existence, and I often found myself just lying around feeling tired. "Resting" became an integral part of my daily routine.

This was not my normal state, but I figured my body was readjusting and it was normal. After another six months, I began getting frustrated by my lack of energy and started talking about it to friends and family. I searched the internet for information on these feelings and came across some reviews I wish so *badly* I had found before my procedure.

I found thousands of reviews on almost every cosmetic procedure you can imagine. You can read the good, the bad, and the ugly about every procedure and every doctor in your area, and see all the before-and-after photos you care to see from thousands of women and men who generously share their stories and intimate details of their experiences.

I started reading voraciously and found out I was not alone in my achiness post-implant. I didn't want to make a big deal out of nothing and was still hopeful everything would work itself out over time, so I just read, researched, and kept to my normal routine as much as possible. Exercise was basically out of the question for me at this point. I had been a jogger and a practicing yoga student three times per week. The achy feeling and painful joint sensations put an end to my jogging, but I managed to keep up with some gentle yoga classes about once per week.

I also spent hours in the hot tub at my gym. I remember the curious looks I would get from fellow gym members as I sat in front of the jets, letting the pulsating water massage my back, shoulders, joints, elbows, wrists, knees, and ankles for hours at a time. Nothing felt as good as that massage. When no one was looking, I also let the water pulsate over my sore breasts and my groin, which has become swollen and puffy over time. I learned later that there are many lymph nodes there. Mine were definitely affected and unhappy. The only thing that felt good was the massaging water or an actual body massage, which seemed to help work things through.

This went on for another year or so before I reached my pain and denial threshold.

Lying in bed one morning without any desire to move because the pain was so intense that it hurt to even stand up, I finally had to admit that something was seriously wrong. I could barely move my arms and legs without severe discomfort. Everything hurt. My body ached with my denial.

For months I had been telling myself that the pain and discomfort would go away, that my body just needed more time to heal, that it would work itself out, and I would soon feel fine . . . and sexy . . . and all the things the breast implant brochure at the surgeon's office alluded to when I went in for my consultation.

That morning, I realized my procedure was not turning out like the brochure, and I needed to take action. I had put on over

20 pounds in the previous two years due to my lack of regular activity. Of course, our sex life had taken a downturn as well, so food had become a solace and comfort to my otherwise pain-ridden body. I was overweight, in pain, and not feeling sexy at all. In fact, my life felt like the exact opposite of the dream promised in the brochure. I felt worse than I had ever felt in my life.

I called the doctor's office to schedule an implant removal consultation. It has been two full years, and I had reached my limit of waiting for everything to work itself out. Unfortunately, the doctor I had seen was retiring, so he was unable to do the removal. He recommended another well-regarded local surgeon and sent me on my way.

The next doctor was not as enthusiastic about the removal process as I was hoping he would be. He told me breast implants are "a one-way street" and that I would not be happy with their appearance if I took them out at this point. He suggested I try a smaller implant and a different brand that, supposedly, had better reviews than the brand I currently had in my body.

He examined me and found that I had experienced a common side effect called capsular contracture, where the body forms a hard shell around the implant as a way to protect itself from the foreign material inside of it. That's why I could no longer sleep on my stomach. My boobs felt like two large baseballs inside my chest. Hard, round, fake pain balls had taken over my chest and left me with the choice to remove them or replace them and try again.

With the guidance of the new doctor and his staff, I chose to replace them and try again with the smaller, newer brand of implant. This was the second worst decision of my life.

The details of the second surgery were not drastically different from the first. Suffice it to say that the procedure prolonged my discomfort with similar symptoms, another round of anesthesia, painkillers, recovery, down time, energy loss, and all the other side effects a surgery has on the body, including another capsular contracture less than a year later. It had now been 3.5 years since my initial implant surgery, and I was mentally and physically exhausted. I called the doctor's office back and said, "I need to take these things out. Can you help me?"

Begrudgingly, the doctor accepted my choice, and we scheduled the removal for the following month.

As I was being rolled into the preoperative area, I found myself in awe. I was in awe of the fact that I had been in this position, not once, not twice, but now three times in the past few years. I was in awe of the fact that *I had chosen this* for myself. Me. A healthy female of sound mind and body *had chosen* to have her body cut open like this without medical necessity. It was purely my vanity that had put me on the table in the operating room three times.

It was *my choice*, and I was in awe of that fact as the doctor strolled in and asked me one last time, "Are you sure you want to do this?" He did not recommend removal and was wary of my final choice. "YES. YES. Take them out! Please. Please take them out!" I was in awe of the fact that he was still asking that question and seemed genuinely confused as to why I would want them taken out. I was relieved as I went under the anesthesia for the third time, only because this time, I knew it would be my last.

· · · · ·

When I woke up in the recovery room, I instantly felt lighter and happier. I looked down at my tightly wrapped gauze covered chest. "Are they gone? Are they really gone?" I asked the nurse gleefully. Yes, they were gone. Relieved, I went home after a couple hours in the recovery room and relaxed in my bed.

Granted, maybe it was the Valium they gave me again to help with the recovery pain, but I felt great. I felt *free*. Literally, the weight had been lifted from my chest, and I was *free*. Not only of the implants but free of all the old ideas I had been carrying about my body, free of my old misconceptions about beauty and what that means and looks like in my female form. I was free of the bullshit the media had been feeding me since I was a young girl about how I should look and how I *should* feel about myself based on my appearance.

I was free of it all and so thankful I had removed this toxic substance, literally and figuratively, from my body, my mind, and my life.

My saga of self-discovery through pain and discomfort was complete, and I was never going back. I was never going back to a mindset that allowed outside influences to affect my view of myself, my body, my beauty, and my value and worth as a woman.

I have no judgment of women who choose to do whatever procedures they want to feel their best. I share this story in the hopes that you, the reader of this chapter, realize you don't *need* to do anything to feel beautiful. Beauty is an inside job.

We all have our journey to live out. My hope is that your journey leads you down the path of self-love. If not yet, I beg you, start today. It took me seven years of intense mental and physical discomfort to find this path and stop comparing myself to celebrities and magazine models. I mean, I still glance at cover models while I'm in the checkout line at the grocery store. The difference is that when I look away now, I know I am enough just as I am. And that is the most beautiful feeling in the world.

## APPLYING THE LESSONS

1. Take a few minutes to appreciate your own body right now. Thank it for all the miraculous things it does for you every day. Close your eyes and feel your breath moving in and out of your lungs. Feel your heart beating. Feel the warmth of your skin. Notice your muscles moving to lift this book up and down. Think of a beautiful sunset you've seen and appreciate your eyes that saw that beauty. Think of your favorite song and appreciate your ears that heard that music.

Think of a fun night of dancing and appreciate your arms and legs, which moved effortlessly to rhythms you could feel in your bones. Thank those bones, too. Maybe they aren't the slender, tall, framing bones of a supermodel, but they work for you. They do their job! Maybe your breasts in a bikini don't turn heads at the beach, but that's not what they are there for anyway.

They nurture young. They are miraculous factories. When we appreciate our bodies for the miraculous things they do for us every day, this is where real beauty dwells.

Look in the mirror and see you own beauty. Your body Is divine. It is your soul's vessel. It allows you to experience the richness of life with all your senses. Your body lets you taste, touch, feel, hear, see, and smell all the fabulous gifts life has to offer you, each and every day. The way it looks is just icing on the cake.

1.  Rather than mentally listing of all your body's imperfections, make a list of all the ways it serves you. Make a list of all the ways you can use that service to make the world around you more beautiful.

Make your list and take one action step in that direction. That's what I call "getting a little work done" in all the right places. This is the work which will deeply improve your quality of life on more than a superficial level.

So, let's get to work ladies. Go ahead. Get a lot of work done! I am planning a full renovation, this time from the inside out rather than the other way around.

# finding your voice

## RACHEL BROWNLOW LUND

"There are ants in the pool," I shouted over to my mom as I squished a dead ant body between my fingers, pulling it off my arm.

*"Aaaannndd . . . of course it would bite me,"* I thought to myself, sourly. Still reeling from a painful breakup, I had spent the last few weeks alternating between ugly crying on the couch and shutting myself in my office, where—more often than I care to admit—I'd while away my time moping, ruminating, and Facebook-stalking my ex.

In an effort to break my pitiful pattern, I'd finally gotten off the couch, made the three-hour drive to visit family in Houston, and swapped my pajamas for a swimsuit. And right as I was beginning to enjoy myself, this happens?

*"Fucking ants,"* I thought, angrily.

I swam a few more laps before pausing again to scratch my arm. Then I scratched my other arm. And then my stomach. Suddenly, my entire body was on fire, burning and itching.

"I need to lie down," I said, barely toweling off before heading inside the house and collapsing on the floor, frantically scratching myself. "Mom, I think you need to take me to the emergency room. I can't breathe."

Soon, I was at Urgent Care, swallowing an antihistamine while epinephrine shot through my body to combat my closing airways.

"You're going to be fine," said the doctor. "I suspect it's more likely an allergy to ant venom than chlorine, but you'll need to get tested to be certain. I recommend that you schedule an appointment with an allergist once you're home."

So I did. Sure enough, an extensive skin prick test confirmed the Urgent Care doctor's theory—I'd developed a severe allergic reaction to imported fire ant venom.

"Allergies aren't predictable," explained my first allergist when I asked him how I could suddenly be deathly allergic to ants when I'd grown up in Texas and never experienced abnormal reactions. "Sometimes you can get bitten 99 times but develop an allergy on the hundredth," he said with a shrug. "Have you experienced higher levels of stress recently?"

Had I ever! Earlier that year, after a tough conversation about whether or not we wanted to have kids together, I'd cut ties with a guy who I'd thought might be "The One." It was the first time since I was 16 that I'd been single for longer than a month, and—I'll be honest—I was not taking it well.

When I wasn't blowing through boxes of tissues, I was working long hours building my ghostwriting company and overseeing a team of writers creating content for small business owners and other influencers.

I'd started my business during college, and it was a personal point of pride for me that I'd grown it from a freelance operation into a respected ghostwriting company that created nonfiction books, articles, and other content for business owners positioning themselves as thought leaders.

My first few years as an entrepreneur presented a steep learning curve; but over time, I became skilled at marketing, positioning, and leveraging connections, as well as tapping into someone else's story, voice, and emotions. As a ghostwriter, I learned the art of reading between the lines to pull forward stories and messages that would not only resonate with readers but also propel the authors and their businesses to greater levels of success.

It took several years to grow the business, but eventually my company reached a level of success that prompted well-known publications like CNNMoney to reach out for interviews.

The attention was fun, but what meant even more to me was being able to provide for myself and the writers on my team.

I still carried with me the childhood memories of feeling less than other students who showed up to school with new, name-brand clothes and giant packs of crayons. Though it had been years since my days of free and reduced-price school lunches, I vividly remembered the embarrassment of standing beside my mom in the grocery store checkout line, wishing the world would swallow me whole as she handed over a stack of food stamps and coupons to pay for our marked-down items and on-clearance produce.

Growing up, I'd heard repeatedly that hard work was the key to success, and to win you had to be the best at something. Now that I was an entrepreneur, I was determined not to go back to a life of scarcity. To prove it, I was working long, grueling hours and holding myself to impossible standards.

I'd internalized messages of perfectionism and endless striving, and while they'd perhaps served me when I'd first entered the world of entrepreneurship, the sustained stress I'd been putting on myself mentally and emotionally had finally caught up with me. Compounded with the recent breakup, the stress had manifested in a deadly allergy to one of Texas's most ubiquitous insects.

## DOCTOR'S ORDERS

It may sound strange, since entrepreneurs are notorious rule-breakers, but at this point in my life I was still very much a play-by-the-rules type of girl. And as every good girl knows, the key to a speedy recovery is to follow your doctor's advice.

For the next few months, I underwent immunotherapy treatment twice a week in an effort to desensitize myself to the point where an ant bite wouldn't end me.

Unfortunately, finding that elusive, nonfatal dosage proved to be more challenging than anticipated. At each session, the allergist would inject me with smaller and smaller doses of venom, hoping to find an amount minute enough that my body would not respond with hives and anaphylaxis.

"This is about 1/100th the potency of a typical bite," said the allergist, preparing his needle for injection. "The smallest dose we can administer. Nothing to worry about. It's basically as if an ant looked at you from across the room."

My body reacted.

"What do I do now?" I asked the doctor.

"My suggestion?" he said, "You're young. It might be time to seriously consider moving. There are no ants farther up north, once you cross the freeze line."

I considered moving away from Texas, the only home I'd ever known. What would it be like to live so far away from my parents, whom I was used to seeing regularly? To leave all my friendships and the contacts I'd worked so hard to cultivate? To leave my life as I knew it, all because of . . . ants?

Soon after, I transferred to a new allergist. But when he, too, gave me the same "move across the freeze line" advice, I did something I hadn't done in quite some time: I listened to my intuition.

Even with doctors telling me otherwise, a small inner voice of wisdom told me there had to be another option; this wasn't the end of my life in Texas. "Someday," the voice told me, "you'll be able to walk outside barefoot again and go on outdoor picnics without risking your life."

## EXPANDING WORLDS

Against my doctors' advice, I stopped seeing allergists altogether and instead upped my safety precautions. My roommate and I had the yard sprayed for ants, and together we developed a more fastidious routine to keep our home crumb-free.

Each time I stepped outside—whether to retrieve the mail, get in my car, or go for a walk—I'd dress in close-toed shoes, sometimes wearing high socks or tall boots for extra layers of protection. All the while, I'd keep my eyes planted firmly on the ground.

My world got smaller, but it continued. Then, one day, as I was driving home, I received a call that changed my life.

A good friend and her husband could no longer care for their three-year-old yorkie, Hans. "We don't want to take him to the animal shelter, if at all possible. Do you know anyone who might want to adopt him?"

"I think I do," I blurted out.

It was a gut reaction. Just months earlier, I'd told my ex that a dog would be too much added responsibility. But Hans? Hans was different. I'd known Hans since he was a hyper-energetic puppy, jumping on couches and eagerly licking people's faces. Since he was little, I'd been dubbed "Aunt Rachel" —the one to watch him while my friends were out of town.

After I adopted Hans, I became "Mom Rachel." And with eight pounds of love added to my life, my world grew a little bigger.

One day, as my roommate and I were walking our dogs around our neighborhood, the unthinkable happened: Hans stepped into an ant mound.

In moments, he was covered with dozens of ants, assailed from every angle.

"Rach, stand back!" said my roommate, as she plucked Hans away from the mound and began pulling the insects off his body, receiving several bites in the process.

I looked on, horrified and fearful. My dog-child was in pain, and all I could do was watch the scene unfold, helplessly.

With the animal hospital and a baby Benadryl on our side, Hans survived, but my confidence in my ability to avoid fire ants had plummeted. How could I be a good dog-mom if I couldn't safely take my dog for walks? Or rescue him from danger?

Moving above the freeze line wasn't the right answer, but neither was avoidance. Adopting Hans had put my health in a different light. I realized my ant allergy didn't affect only me. Others were now dependent on my health as well, and I did not want to let them down. I wanted more for my life. And that's when I got curious.

## CHOOSING CURIOSITY

For years, I'd been interested in health and wellness, and now my allergy prompted me to examine how they intersected with my mindset, fear, and self-doubt. Gradually, I began to immerse myself in independent study, learning about chakras, energy work, metaphysics, and self-care. I also examined my relationship with myself, realizing how trapped I'd been in toxic patterns of perfectionism, comparisonitis, anxiety, and workaholism.

As I continued, I learned about spiritual teacher Louise Hay's powerful work around health, healing, and happiness and how thoughts have the power to create one's reality. At the end of her book, *You Can Heal Your Life*, she includes a list of physical ailments and probable emotional thought patterns behind individual health issues.

When I read her findings on allergies, I got goosebumps. According to Hay, the probable mental and emotional cause behind allergies is denying one's own power. And wow, had I been denying!

Since I was little, I'd wanted to be a published author. However, even with an English degree and more than a dozen written books under my belt, none was in my own name. Instead, I was a writer without a byline. A ghost. The person behind others' successes.

While there are financial benefits to ghostwriting, continuing on that path had kept me playing small, denying my power and my voice. It was a way of playing safe and hiding from the world. I feared I didn't have anything of my own important enough to say, and those fears were preventing me from sharing my thoughts. It felt safer not to put myself out there than to risk rejection and ridicule.

In a flash, I also realized I was denying my power to be strong and resilient on my own. I'd been dating boys who weren't right for me and explaining away their bad behavior—from cheating to emotional manipulation to drug use—in an effort to keep the peace.

Even outside of romantic relationships, it had become commonplace for me to disregard my inner voice of wisdom; instead, I'd go out of my way to make others feel comfortable. I'd always been highly empathetic, but by pushing back my inner wisdom and putting my well-being on the backburner, I was denying my power.

When these realizations struck, I knew I had to take action, imperfect as it may be. And so, as uncomfortable as it was, I slowly but steadily began leaning into my power and speaking up.

I closed the book-writing side of my company and began taking more assignments that would let me claim my voice. I joined Toastmasters and began writing and giving my own speeches. To get to know myself better, I put dating on hold and promised myself I would be single for at least a year. And after researching local intuition teachers, I began working with a woman who taught me how to look inside myself for answers and trust my inner guidance.

It was a magical time of self-transformation. I found that the more I lived with intention and honored my intuition, the more secure and confident I became. And the more secure and confident I became, the more my business and life flourished.

No longer was I working weekends and pulling all-nighters to complete assignments clients had requested last-minute. Instead, I established firmer boundaries around work hours and raised prices for rush jobs. I stopped mentally beating myself up for my every shortcoming and instead offered myself love and compassion.

## THOUGHTS CREATE THINGS

About a year into this new intentional life, I sensed something in me had shifted. On a mind, body, and soul level, I felt healthier than I had in years. That'sAp when the thought fluttered through my mind, *"What if I'm no longer allergic?"*

A few months later, the thought changed: *"I'm no longer allergic."*

While I wasn't about to stand atop an ant mound to test my theory, I began telling a few close friends and family that I had a feeling I had healed myself of my ant allergy.

"I'm glad you're feeling better," they'd reply, "Just keep your EpiPen on you, so I don't have to worry."

So I did.

Then, one summer, I got bitten.

I'd been told that, in the event of an ant bite, I should administer the necessary medication and dial 911 immediately so that a trained professional could observe my symptoms.

I'd be lying if I said I didn't experience any fear when that ant struck, but my more prominent emotion was curiosity. This was my chance to learn whether or not my body had truly healed itself.

And so, reckless by some standards and brave by others, I held off on self-administering and instead observed my body's reaction. With curiosity, I watched as the site of the swelling grew a bit larger than normal and then . . . stopped. No other hives appeared, and my breathing remained normal.

Since then, I've had several more encounters with fire ants (including getting bitten by a jumbo-sized ant in Kenya) and while I have a healthy respect for them, I no longer fear them. It's funny how something so small can be so life-changing.

## APPLYING THE LESSONS

It's important to remember that everyone is going through their own struggles. Sometimes—as with my ant allergy—a person can appear to be healthy and thriving on the outside, but behind the scenes, they are coping with invisible illnesses, trapped emotions, and limiting beliefs. Whatever you're going through right now, know that you are not alone. There are people, resources, and the support you need to get past whatever may be troubling you.

Sometimes the learning is part of the journey. With that said, I'll share a few practices which helped me heal my body and my life:

## 1. Hone your intuition with muscle testing.

One of the best things I've ever done for my life was to hire an intuition teacher to teach me how to tap into my inner wisdom to make powerful decisions that are in my best interest.

Before I learned how to do this, I often made decisions based on what I thought would be the "right" thing to do, rather than what my heart, gut, or body told me was my truth.

When I was tired, I'd work through the exhaustion; and when I was sick, I'd work through the pain. If I had a decision to make, I'd base it on what I thought I "should" do instead of tapping in to discover what would be in my best interest.

Learning how to tap into my intuition allowed me to begin trusting myself in a way I'd never before been able to do. It instilled in me a deeper confidence in myself and helped me to become an even stronger and more successful business owner and leader.

While there are many methods of receiving intuitive information, one of the most readily accessible to novices and intuitive masters alike is muscle testing.

Our bodies inherently know what is in our best interest and what is not. When muscle testing, they become strong in response to positive stimulus, and they become weak in response to negative stimulus.

Because muscle testing is such a powerful way to tap into the body's inner wisdom, more and more coaches, chiropractors, and nutritionists are using it in their practices. It's something I often teach my clients and something I'd like to teach you as well. Read on to discover how to perform the sway test, one of the simplest forms of muscle testing.

### Setting the scene

Sit upright, and close your eyes. For this exercise, there should be no chairback behind you.

### Testing and calibrating

Before asking for real intuitive information, I recommend performing a simple calibration test to determine how your body indicates a "yes" and how it indicates a "no."

For example, you may say aloud, "My name is [insert your first name]."

Sit in quiet awareness, and notice how your body receives this information. If you said your actual name in your calibration test, then you may have noticed your torso shift ever so slightly. Most people experience a subtle shift forward for accurate/yes responses and backward for inaccurate/no responses.

Now try the test again, but this time with a name that is not your own. Example: "My name is [insert a name that is not your own]." Now notice: Did your body shift forward or backward?

It's important to test both true and false responses to accurately calibrate.

It may take a couple tries to begin picking up on the subtle shifts. However, after you begin noticing them, they will become easier to detect.

### Ask for real information

Once you've asked your calibration questions and have received satisfactory responses, you are ready to use the sway test to receive actual information.

Our bodies naturally know whether something is true or false and whether it is good for us or not.

There are an unlimited number of yes-or-no questions you can get answers to using the say test. Here are a few to get you started:

- "It's in my best interest to ____."

- "Doing ＿＿ will positively impact my business."

- "＿＿ is healthy for me."

- "My relationship with ＿＿ is negatively impacting my health."

As you continue to practice muscle testing, your body's responses will become clearer. Master this method, and not only will it cut down your decision fatigue dramatically, but it will also improve your life.

## 2. Raise your vibration.

Along my woo-woo journey, as I affectionately like to call it, I learned the spiritual principles of energy and frequency. Simply put, energy is at the most fundamental levels of everything in the universe, from the food we eat to the chairs we sit on to ourselves. That energy can vibrate at a high frequency (think: peace, joy, love, enlightenment) or at a low frequency (think: shame, guilt, apathy, grief).

Because like energy attracts like energy, those who vibrate at higher frequencies tend to attract other people and opportunities that vibrate at similar frequencies, and those at lower frequencies tend to attract low-vibrating people and opportunities.

Some of the fastest and most effective ways I've found to raise my vibration include maintaining a daily gratitude journal; receiving massage and energy healings; staying well hydrated; eating high-quality, organic foods; surrounding myself with other high-vibe people; and exercising.

There are going to be times when your vibration is down and you're going to feel scared and unsure of yourself. In those times, it helps to have a high-vibrating support system around you to lift you up and cheer for you.

For me, adopting and caring for a dog was a big part of my self-healing journey. It allowed me to pour my love and nurturing into another being without immediately jumping into another romantic or codependent relationship. In return, I received unconditional love and another reason to go outside for sunshine and daily exercise.

If this all sounds a bit woo-woo to you, I completely understand. I was super skeptical when I first encountered these ideas, but once I began reading the science behind it and witnessing the research proven out in my own life, I stopped resisting. Why resist if it works?

(Note: for a more data-driven explanation of these principles, read *Power vs. Force: The Hidden Determinants of Human Behavior* by David R. Hawkins, M.D., Ph.D.)

### 3. Concentrate on lead indicators, not lag indicators.

When you're building something big, whether it's a new business, better health, or a budding relationship, there will be moments when the results you're getting are not yet measuring up to all of the time and energy you're putting in to get them.

When this happens, I've learned it's best to focus on the process and disconnect from the results.

In business, we use the terms "lead indicators" and "lag indicators" to differentiate the outputs that contribute to results from the results themselves. Lead indicators are all of the actions and efforts that go into the process, while lag indicators are typically the big results you're hoping to manifest.

It can be easy to concentrate on lag indicators or those big end goals; but I encourage you to keep those small actions front and center. They add up!

If you're showing up daily, tapping into your intuition, maintaining a high vibration, and working your plan, you will find success.

Sometimes you're not going to have all the answers laid out in front of you. Doubt, fear of the unknown, or other limiting beliefs may creep in. Perhaps you'll be going through so much already that it feels overwhelming to move forward.

When that happens, know this: *YOU CAN DO IT!* All you need to know is the best next step. Do one thing today that will propel you forward, and tomorrow, do something else.

Focus on those lead indicators, and you WILL grow your confidence, your inner strength, and your voice.

Small, consistent actions add up. Those consistent actions have the power to change your life, and you—yes, you!—have the power to create massive change and positively impact the world.

# living a life in balance

## RACHEL ZIERZOW

"I'm sorry to have to tell you this, but you probably won't be able to have children. It seems as if you're going through what is called early menopause." As I sat in the gynecologist's office under the fluorescent lights where I had gone for a routine exam, I felt alone, shocked, and grief-stricken. I was only 29 years old.

At the time, my calendar was full of doctor appointments, my medicine cabinet was littered with prescription medications, and I had a huge binder with all my notes to keep track of it all. I was suffering from leaky gut syndrome, IBS, chronic fatigue, stomach ulcers, bouts of anxiety and depression, seasonal allergies, recurring asthma and bronchitis, tendonitis, carpal tunnel syndrome, tooth decay, and menstrual problems. Even with good access to medical care, I felt like I was falling apart, crashing into a downward spiral. I remember wondering how long it would be before I hit rock bottom.

Through the years I searched for a doctor who could fix my problems, or at least get my symptoms under control. But when I received the "early menopause" diagnosis, I suddenly yearned to know the root cause of my illness and was determined to take full responsibility for my health. No more doctors, no more pills. I refused to accept, at age 29, that I would never have children.

As I struggled with my health, I was still fully functioning with a full-time job, a hobby of long-distance running and triathlons, and a new marriage. In order to keep up with the pace of life and appear somewhat healthy, I took antibiotics, painkillers, antacids, cough medicine, muscle relaxants, allergy medications, and stronger prescriptions when needed. I was treating the symptoms, but hadn't uncovered the root cause of my illnesses.

I was well-practiced at burning the candle at both ends. Throughout high school and college, I spread myself thin with athletics, music, academics, and social activities, making plans far into the future so nothing would fall to chance. I always got straight A's. I needed approval and wanted everyone to like me. I kept super busy so that I wouldn't have to confront the insecurity, sadness, and depression that lurked beneath the surface.

Halfway through my 29th year, I came down with a bad case of bronchitis. It was Memorial Day weekend, and doctors' offices were closed. I took cough syrup and whatever else I could find to get me through until Tuesday. That was a mistake. My lungs were so congested that I broke several ribs in violent coughing episodes.

I was scared to death, fearing I might not be able to take another breath. I remember kneeling on the floor, hunched over my bed, begging the universe for help. "Please, God, just tell me what I need to do to heal. Point me in the right direction. I'll do anything."

· · · · ·

A short time later, at dinner with friends, I shared how I was searching for the root cause of my illnesses. A friend mentioned he had been enjoying eating at a vegan, macrobiotic restaurant near downtown Austin called Casa de Luz and recommended it to help with my health issues. I was intrigued and went a few days later.

Casa de Luz is unlike any restaurant I'd ever been to. A beautiful walkway with lush, tropical plants and wind chimes led to the entrance. Inside, a lovely, peaceful atmosphere welcomed me, and a yoga school and school of natural cooking shared the restaurant's campus.

Over the next few months, I went more and more often to Casa de Luz, started a daily yoga practice, and attended a free lecture given by the cooking school titled "How Foods Affect Your Health and Emotions." I started making connections between how I felt and what I consumed—not just food, but also daily activities, media, and relationships. Instead of pushing through the pain or popping antacids or pain killers to "fix" the problem, I started listening. Little by little, I began to understand what was making me sick.

Just after turning 30, I signed up for a weekend intensive at Natural Epicurean Academy of Culinary Arts called "The Fundamentals of Macrobiotic Cooking for Disease Prevention and Reversal." I remember thinking I already knew how to cook, but might learn a thing or two to help me with my health issues. I laugh at myself now, because I actually had so much to learn!

The minute I walked through the door for the workshop, I realized I had stumbled on something magical. I was mesmerized as I stood watching the cooking school owner, Dawn, and her student assistants slice, dice, and chop evenly and efficiently, cooking in a variety of styles with what seemed like little effort. They were not only proficient and skilled, but they seemed happy, healthy, and integrated into a community focused on healing.

That day I learned how to use a chef's knife—how to hold it, sharpen it, and properly dice an onion, a carrot, a winter squash, and so on. We made many kinds of soup, whole grains, vegetables, and sea vegetables, using Le Creuset pots and bamboo utensils, and assembled them into beautiful meals.

We cooked with healing foods I didn't know existed, like kabocha squash, daikon radish, lotus root, miso, ume plum vinegar, dried shiitake mushrooms, barley, millet, quinoa, adzuki beans, and kombu, to name just a few. Maybe I was following in the footsteps of my great-grandmother, Edith Zierzow, who cooked huge farm-to-table meals daily for everyone working at her Wisconsin farm.

Growing up, my diet was not so varied. I ate a few veggies like peas, carrots, broccoli, and occasionally green beans from my mother's garden. But I also consumed bowls of ice cream, soft drinks, potato chips, and processed cereal on a daily basis. By the time I was in second and third grade, I'd started to gain excess weight and suffered from allergies, tooth decay, and colds. My vision began deteriorating, and I even felt some anxiety and depression, although I didn't know what it was at the time. These were early signs of a growing imbalance in my internal environment. I didn't have the foundation I needed for solid, robust health as a teenager and adult.

In my teens and early twenties, I was treated with antibiotics for acne prevention, was prescribed heavy doses of antibiotics for parasites contracted while studying abroad in South America, and took all kinds of other medications for colds, stomachaches, and pain. All these medicines were aimed at short-term relief of symptoms but didn't address the underlying issues and took me further away from balance.

Back at the Natural Epicurean, I attended lectures on creating balance in my everyday life, achieving acid-alkaline balance in the diet, and looking at life through the lens of opposing energies—yin (expansive energy) and yang (contractive energy). These were fundamental ways of looking at my life and the world that I hadn't known about before.

As my fellow students and I sat down for our first meal together, I knew I was hooked. While eating the creamy kabocha squash soup, I felt deeply nourished, as if every cell in my body was soaking up healing energy. I knew there was no turning back. The next day I signed up for the Natural Epicurean's program in macrobiotic studies and natural foods cooking. I had no idea at the time that this decision would be the beginning of a long journey of healing and transformation of both my body and my career.

Over the next three years, I studied at the Natural Epicurean on nights and weekends and cooked at home every chance I got, to practice what I was learning. Meanwhile, I still had my day job as a learning specialist at the university, which I had begun after getting my master's degree in ecology and evolution. This was the "stable job with benefits" I thought I needed to be a responsible adult. But to me, it represented my failure to make it in the cut-throat academic world as a biology professor.

Although the job was varied with lots of interaction with students and competent, good-hearted colleagues, before graduate school, my dream was to become a biology professor, not a learning specialist. I wanted to teach students about the beauty and wonder of the natural world, in hopes of inspiring them to do conservation and environmental protection work. After almost four years swimming upstream in the Ph.D. program in a male-dominated science department without a suitable mentor, I was completely discouraged. I wrote up the research I had done so far and left with a master's degree.

Although I should have been proud of my accomplishment, my self-confidence was at an all-time low, and I grasped for things in my life to give me a boost. I found the learning specialist job, ended my relationship (I felt like I literally had nothing to offer), and took up running again to meet people and get exercise.

In retrospect, I see that I was literally running from my problems, trying to keep myself busy and distracted. My health issues were worsening by the day. I simply did not have the energy or drive to follow my dreams.

While working as a learning specialist, I had a student assistant named Ja who worked in my office several days a week. Ja was born in China and came to the U.S. with her parents when she was six years old, living in various places before finally settling in a small town near Houston at age 14.

Ja learned from her parents how to work hard and started college on a full scholarship at age 15. She immediately declared her major as pre-med, in line with her lifelong dream of becoming a doctor. On the fast track to becoming a medical doctor, she studied hard but also made time for friends, social events, and volunteering.

Ja was vibrant, fun-loving, intelligent, confident, and idealistic and always had a smile on her face. She seemed to be going through life fearlessly, confronting challenges head-on, and refusing to listen to anything that would discourage her from her dreams.

At 18, things were really lining up for her, personally and academically. I must admit I was jealous. I recalled the days of feeling young and idealistic, before graduate school, but those days were long gone for me.

During my frequent chats with Ja, I often refrained from praising her efficient work and sparkling personality, instead making small talk about her friends and activities. I asked her what she was doing for spring break, and she told me she was going to a conference in Dallas for physicians and pre-med students. She would travel up there with a carload of her classmates (including her new fiancé) and make a vacation out of it.

When I got to work on the Monday of spring break, a coworker broke the tragic news that Ja had died in a car accident on her way to the conference just days before. A tractor-trailer crossed over the median strip on the highway and collided with their vehicle, causing a fatal accident. I was in total shock and didn't want to believe it.

Maybe the newspaper got the information wrong, maybe she was in the hospital, already on her way to recovery? Could she and her friends have been misidentified? I felt panic, then pain, and started thinking of her parents, friends, and teachers.

A week later, I went to the funeral in Ja's hometown. I got to talk with her mother, who seemed so young, frail, and emotionally distraught. On the tortuous three-hour car ride home, with nowhere to escape, my heart broke into pieces. I couldn't stop crying for days. It didn't make sense.

In the midst of this tragedy, I started seeing things more clearly. I felt the kind, vibrant spirit of my young friend beginning to work on me in the weeks to come. It felt like I had new lenses to look through. Before Ja's death, I was unconsciously going through the motions of living, without allowing myself to feel, dream, or be inspired to make real changes in my life. Even though I was almost done with the transformational course at the Natural Epicurean, I hadn't made my move. I was afraid of taking a leap and following my dreams. At that moment, I felt determined to use Ja's life as an inspiration for moving forward with mine.

Six months later, I quit my safe, comfortable university job, propelled by a force much greater than myself. I started my business of healing personal chef work, cooking for a family expecting their first child and for an elderly couple who had just discovered the healing power of macrobiotics. I also started teaching at the Natural Epicurean and began studying to be a macrobiotics health counselor at Macrobiotics America.

Sadly, within a few months, I separated from my husband of three years. Within weeks of our separation, I met the man who would become the father of my child. Four years after I had been told that I would never have children, I gave birth to a beautiful baby girl who was born with a kind, generous soul.

At age 36, I became the lead instructor of macrobiotics at the Natural Epicurean, guiding hundreds of students through the professional chef training program until its closing in 2017. I also kept working with individuals through holistic health counseling and healing chef work and saw my health improve steadily over time. I'm grateful my illnesses and symptoms of the past are no longer with me today.

In 2016 I married my husband, Nelson, who is an amazing stepfather to my daughter and my biggest supporter in being an entrepreneur and sharing my experience of healing with others.

Now, at age 45, I look back at my healing journey and realize that it's all about balance. Rather than trying to balance out one extreme with another, I opt for choices that are closer to the middle. Instead of a restrictive diet (or high-stress junk food), I make choices about what to eat based on how I feel, what my body needs seasonally, and what gives me the most strength and vitality. Instead of long-distance running, I take walks on the greenbelt, do gentle yoga, swim in the springs, and play with my family. Instead of judging and criticizing myself, I practice accepting and forgiving myself on a daily basis.

It takes time to unwind and change destructive habits and patterns. But it is empowering to know that we have choices, and when we make choices that are in alignment with our truth, we will thrive.

I used to define success as a prestigious graduate degree, a fancy job title, or a high salary. Although I want my business to continue to grow and be successful, I already know I'm on the right track. I was able to change the trajectory of my life, improve my health, have a family, and be truly content with what I have. The work I have been fortunate to do for 12 years now, working with individuals and groups to improve their lives through healthy, balanced living, has blessed me with amazing friends and a large, supportive community of healers.

## APPLYING THE LESSONS

No matter where you are on your healing journey, this is the perfect time to take care of yourself and make choices which will support you to the fullest. Here are some practical steps to help you along the way:

### 1. Love and accept yourself, with all your gifts and imperfections.

When making your to-do list, put "Love myself" at the top of the list, which means to sprinkle things throughout the day which nourish you and make you happy. If you tend to take care of others at your own expense, start changing that reflex. Pause when you have the thought to help someone (who probably hasn't even asked for your help), and consider doing something to care for yourself instead. At the end of the day, write down three things you did well that day. When you look in the mirror, compliment yourself as you would your best friend or your child.

### 2. Nourish yourself with fresh food, kind people, and gifts of nature.

Get outside where you can see trees and green, which helps to reduce stress and pressure. Walk barefoot in the grass or on the beach—it is grounding and benefits your overall health and immune system. Make a big pot of soup each week that you can warm up throughout the week. Soups are deeply nourishing, easy to digest, and full of minerals. Spend time with people who make you feel good rather than with those who drain your energy. Seek out relationships with people who are also on a healing path and who have gained wisdom from their journey.

**3. Make decisions each day which are in alignment with your inner knowing.**

Pay attention to the signals your body gives you. If something doesn't feel right in your core area—if you feel tight, queasy, or uneasy there—it is not the right thing to do. Walk away and reevaluate. Listening to your body is key to making good decisions.

**4. Slow down the pace of life so that you can make time to care for yourself.**

Instead of overscheduling your days, try blocking out some time each day for yourself, even if it is just five minutes here and there. This is the perfect time for self-care, such as sitting quietly for a few minutes to meditate, taking a salt bath with essential oils, getting a haircut, having lunch with a friend, making yourself a home-cooked meal, taking a nap, or whatever else makes you happy.

Try one or more of these steps for one day, one week, or one month and notice how things shift in your life. Maybe you will be able to finally launch your business or ask for the raise you deserve, or maybe your life will take on an exciting new direction! Perhaps you will see things more clearly, find a wonderful new collaborator, or discover how best to align your business with your values.

It is never too late to start living a life in balance, no matter where you are on your healing journey. With practice, nourishing acts will become habits, which will have a profound impact on your life. The most important thing is to be kind and gentle with yourself. Encourage yourself to continue with your healthy, nourishing practices, even after you stray for a while. Being true to ourselves and opening up to people and resources will help each one of us fulfill our life's purpose.

# manifesting my magic through miracles

## DR. ROSE ANNE MULLIGAN

Narcissism, alcoholism, drug use, verbal and physical abuse, anxiety, depression, and suicidal fantasies were our family portrait. Every member of my family was deep in their own version of dysfunction, pain and suffering we somehow all took out on ourselves and each other. This was all I knew and yet I knew there had to be more.

I was born into an Irish Catholic family in a small coalmining town in northeastern Pennsylvania. The younger of two daughters, I grew up in my grandmother's home on a street with time-worn flagstone sidewalks that were pushed up here and there by the oaks, maples, and sycamores. Each season was reminiscent of a postcard: early spring flowers for Easter, fireworks and cookouts for the 4th of July, the most dazzling foliage change in the fall, and in winter, Christmas lights, snowmen, and presents.

Like many other families, we said, "I love you," yet somehow it seemed the actions never quite matched the words. Love is as love does, I hold true now in my life, and although we spoke of love and showed affection, deep down, I thought those who loved each other should treat each other better.

As young as four years old, I always felt something was very wrong. I felt anxiety daily and woke up most mornings terrified and sick to my stomach. I often felt sad and alone, and I was painfully shy. It was very scary for me to make friends and to extend trust in my youth. Trust starts at home, and I felt there was no one there whom I could trust.

At that age, I was too young to understand PTSD, anxiety, depression, and addictive behaviors, all of which I fell prey to very early in life. As a doctor now, I understand that my nervous system was on high alarm defending against the "invisible tiger" in the room, which at any given moment could be my dissatisfied, drunk father, my frustrated, angry mother, or my resentful, bullying sister.

What I did come to realize very early on that hurt people turn about and hurt people. Monsters are created, not born, and I knew I did not want to become a monster and I wanted to help hurt people.

One day, my parents threw a party in our home for my sister's first holy communion. We seldom had company over to the house, or parties, due to my father's drinking and my mother's intolerance for others, yet that day the house was buzzing with relatives and neighbors. A palpable energy and richness that coursed through our home, and I loved it!

Music, laughter, and celebration filled my home. At that moment, I realized that happiness, joy, and pleasure have the power to set us free and enable us to love ourselves and love one another. I witnessed my own family being taken in by the party. It was wonderful to see my mother smile, my father laugh, and my sister dance and play.

From out of the blue, a beautiful, strong, and gentle voice whispered into my ear, captivating my attention with a statement of the most incredible and unbelievable nature. The "voice" spoke these words: *"You Are Here to Save Humanity."*

What? Save humanity? ME? I was only four! I was taken aback and curious as to what exactly this could mean. And there was no one there, no one around me whispering in my ear. This statement came from the ether. Was I dreaming? Was I hearing things? And I knew this message was for me, and I knew to take it seriously.

Part of me was overwhelmed at how much responsibility this could mean for me; after all, I felt I was a full-time caretaker for my family already. And I was pretty sure my family life was only going to get worse. And a part of me felt deep compassion for those I would be honored to help. Even at that young age, I took pleasure in helping others and had a knowing of life that an average four-year-old might not possess. I was told I was born older than most, and from a very early age, empathy and compassion were my super powers. Still, it was quite a lot to take in.

Even though I was sure and eager for more messages from the beyond, and waited for further instruction, there were no more messages for a long time.

. . . . .

As I grew, stress levels seemed to grow with me each year. With no relief from a deteriorating family life, I soon started to acquire a self-defense strategy of my own. I turned to food to ease my pain.

I often woke very early in the morning before everyone was awake, just to sneak food. I'd steal away and eat whatever I could, and not get caught. I lost all self-control and couldn't help myself. I cultivated a self-loathing that could be eased only momentarily with more eating, which led to more loathing. And so, the cycle perpetuated itself.

Just when I thought life couldn't get any worse, one day my mother had enough of my father's drinking, criticism, and abuse and walked out of our lives without saying goodbye. I felt so abandoned and incredibly frightened. I realized I was more alone than ever.

At 11 years old, what was I to do? My mother had attempted to keep the only semblance of order in the house, and now she was gone. I never told of the bullying from my sister, and my mom always handed off my drunk father to me when he got to be too much for her, so not only was all hell about to break loose, but life as I knew it was to be an ever-waking nightmare for many years to come. So from that moment on, I was in charge of raising myself, trying to care for my ailing alcoholic father, and staying out of the wrath of my out-of-control, mean teenage sister, who was clearly on her own despair- and anger-induced rampage. And trying not to eat everything in sight.

As I grew into the teen years, I was just starting to really comprehend that my family's dysfunction and my eating disorder were serious problems. I began to experience mini "blackouts." Just as I was feeling overwhelmed and had the strong impulse to binge, I would try to reason with myself to stop the act. It was as if time stopped, I blacked out, and then awoke to find that whatever food I was trying to avoid consuming was completely eaten. I felt sad beyond comprehension, doomed and cursed.

I struggled just to make it through each day. Help was not something my family taught me to receive, expect, or ask for, which led me to believe that I had no one to help me and no one to turn to. These were the first years when suicide began to surface as an attractive option.

Still, I continued to remember that voice, and out of seemingly nowhere, I gained courage and wanted to find the determination to succeed. To succeed for myself and to help others find their success. I was resolute and resourceful in finding ways to help myself. I would dance when I was sad, I would go out in nature to be embraced by the trees, I would spend time alone dreaming of a better life. It was the only way I had any hope of staying alive and fulfilling my destiny.

• • • • •

High school was a nightmare, and I was so happy to turn 18, get a job, and set out on my new adventure of finding my awesomeness and create a vocation out of it. I always knew to find something I loved and do that. The business will happen, the money will come, and I will be a success. So I went out to look for something that I would love to do and concurrently be of service.

Despite my addictions—ADD, PTSD, depression, and

anxiety—I applied to Penn State with aspirations to major in psychology. Maybe this was where I was to find answers for my and my family's behavior and to gain knowledge to help myself and, in turn, help others. After all, as the "voice" predicted, helping humanity was my destiny.

My binging, learning difficulties, depression, and suicidal fantasies were accelerated by the pressures of college. I lived at home while in school, and the mad mix of home life and academia became overwhelming. This was a "dark period," as I like to call the episodes when fantasies of my non-existence were inescapable. Suicidal thoughts tormented my mind relentlessly. In an attempt to gain some measure of control of my life and alleviate my pain and despair, and to be able to have control of something, I had reached out to the counseling center at Penn State and found I could only be seen in two weeks. My life was crashing down around me. In my scared disposition and confusion, I just couldn't wait two weeks, so my only recourse was, sadly, dropping out of college.

I'm sure that today screening processes are better for those calling in to counseling centers in colleges. Back then individuals fell through the cracks so much more often. With the stigma and shame of suicide and addictions weighing heavy on me, I isolated further.

I took the next few months to regroup, avoid my family, collect my thoughts, and get back to a place where I could contemplate my reality. I had to get back on track with my mission and seek out answers on my own.

I had no mentors and no family to turn to. This lack of help led me to a Barnes and Noble, looking and hoping for a book that could somehow show me the way. Self-help books were just starting to become popular, and I can thank Louise Hay for being there for me that day. Her books brought me up from despair and gave me faith in myself again. Her words taught me to forgive myself and others; they lifted me up and gave me the confidence to move forward, to love myself and to choose to live.

This was one of the biggest turning points in my life. At that moment, I decided I was going to pursue a self-study of health and wellness of mind, body, and spirit. Keeping physically fit, happy, healthy, and spiritually conscious was my new focus and life raft. I could do this myself, for myself. Loving myself and taking excellent care of me, because I deserve it, is one of the biggest lessons I have learned so far in my life.

I was on a mission to be my very best and to inspire others to do the same. Helping others has always been a passion of mine, even from a very young age. I loved lifting people I met out in the world up, reminding them they are LOVE and that they have and came with the "stuff" they need to be happy, healthy, and joyful, regardless of their circumstances. I wanted to reflect back their perfection so they could own it, rise up, and live their birthright of joy.

I was the friend with the compassionate ear, I was the stranger with the kind word or action that changed courses of lives. I was the joy that was contagious in the world. This brought me even more happiness and pleasure.

Finding this happiness is when I realized I was to take my passion and turn it into a business so that I could thrive and give myself the ability to succeed in life. I felt that if I could lift myself up and transform my life, I could fulfill my prophetic destiny and help others do the same.

This was my new goal and direction. I just didn't, at the time, know how. There was no such thing as a "life coach" back then, so I would have conversations with the "divine forces that be," asking for signs to set me in the direction of making this happen. After all, the voice said I was here to save all of humanity, so I would find a way to elevate my existence and lead the way through suffering to happiness!

• • • • •

This was to be my gift. We've all heard the saying, *There is a gift in every wound.* I was determined to find my gift, heal my wounds, and use my gifts to help others find theirs. Somehow, I knew deep inside that I was cultivating wisdom, which would serve me and others to get to that *other side.* This was now the motivation behind me never giving up on myself.

To that end, I eventually found what I was looking for, or rather, it found me.

Tara, a friend of mine, invited me to a neighborhood dinner talk on health and wellness. I accepted merely in hopes of meeting and making some like-minded friends, hearing some interesting information about the body. and sharing a nice Italian dinner.

Her father, Dr. Claude Lessard, an esteemed practitioner and founder of a chiropractic college, was hosting a talk on the philosophy, art, and science of his work. A special guest speaker and good friend of Dr. Lessard was a world-renowned chiropractor by the name of Dr. Reggie Gold. He spoke of his journey discovering chiropractic and how it became a passion for him to be of service to humanity through this profession.

I was enjoying being there and, in all truthfulness, was just interested in some intellectual philosophizing. It was moving testimony. However, I was not in any way expecting what happened next.

I was taken by surprise as I felt a white-hot flame suddenly course through me. It was of such force and realistic nature that I sat in my chair almost paralyzed and in shock! For what seemed like an eternity, I literally saw, and felt, white flames all around me, from the floor up to the ceiling. It was like something out of a sci-fi movie. It was so powerful and vivid that I thought others near me surely must have witnessed this, too.

It didn't take me long to realize this was a defining sign. It wasn't a voice this time, but rather a vision and fantastic sensation. Do things like this really happen? A white-hot flame of passion is not to be ignored. I immediately investigated becoming a Doctor of Chiropractic.

• • • • •

I knew it would be an uphill battle, with my emotional ups and downs and learning difficulties, but if this choice got me closer to my purpose in life, then I was all in. This would be the medium through which I would serve humanity!

I soon applied and got accepted to Chiropractic University. I was excited to be on my way to becoming a doctor and healer, and my world was wide open for possibilities. I loved learning about the body and learning the different techniques. And yet, I still was looking for my path in all of this and how was I to serve. Destiny knocked on my door again.

Chiropractic education was hard, very hard. The curriculum was dense and extensive--way more than I expected or than many people realize. The credit hours were long, and I found myself slipping into the despair of thinking I couldn't keep up with the demands of Chiropractic college. The dark shadows started to creep in, and I was getting scared, knowing how deep I could slip. I needed another sign or miracle very soon. I couldn't even imagine that I would have to drop out again.

Then one day, the sun came out again in the most unexpected way. Doctors who taught different techniques often came to campus to share their stories and work. One day I was on campus and noticed a flyer announcing a "lunch and learn" with Dr. Donny Epstein. This is where I was introduced to a new, leading-edge body of work and technology called Network Spinal and its sister work, Somato Respiratory Integration (SRI). This technique of chiropractic and breath work was not being taught on any campus at the time due to its "out of the box" approach.

There is a very strong adherence to tradition in the chiropractic educational system. This Network Spinal stuff was new and far from being accepted, much less understood by the establishment. It was considered too avant garde and therefore unwelcome. That piqued my interest!

Dr. Epstein was banned from most campuses at the time. There must have been a greater force of good involved in having him on my campus that day. Mysterious events take place when one is following their dreams and aspirations with a white-hot passion. I was open and receptive to the gifts of the Universe, and it was obvious to me that I was in the exact right place, at the exact right time. It was amazingly serendipitous.

I was enchanted by the thought of learning something so new and groundbreaking that the establishment was upset about its very existence. I've always thought of myself as a pioneer, a forward thinker, and an early adopter. So I was intrigued by Dr. Epstein's work.

What I heard that day was so very different, a huge departure from what I had been exposed to in my chiropractic education up to that point. Dr. Epstein was speaking on the importance of taking into account the whole being of the person, the seen and the unseen factors that make up our humanness, not just spinal biomechanics and physiology. Mind, body, emotions, and spirit were taken into account, and this technique was able to directly connect us to the source of our being in a way that I had never heard of or seen before.

Most people are unaware that the body stores physical, mental, and emotional stress and trauma as vibrations. This is especially evident for those who are under perpetual stress with no time to heal or find resolution, as in those who suffer from PTSD, or for those with no life-coping or healing strategies and support.

Stress is the leading cause of most disease states and is the number one contributor to people's dissatisfaction in their lives. According to the American Psychological Association, chronic stress is linked to the six leading causes of death: heart disease, cancer, lung ailments, accidents, cirrhosis of the liver, and suicide. And more than 75 percent of all physician office visits are for stress-related ailments and complaints.

· · · · ·

Stress bends us out of shape. It manifests in and is evident in our posture. It makes such sense that the shape, tone, and tension of our spine is in direct proportion to and correlates with the shape, tone, and tension of our life. If our spine is out of alignment, we most likely are not living in alignment with our authentic life, for which we were created. This inauthentic life can create pain and suffering that have vast repercussions and consequences for our health. It becomes obvious that a healthy spine equals a healthy life, which sets the stage for you being your very best and sharing that with the world.

With Network Spinal, every cell of your body can respond differently to stress. The gentle, precise touches along the spine cue the brain and central nervous system to reorganize and release the stored stress and tension in the body that inhibit our ability to function, think, heal, feel, and even live optimally. We recycle and reuse the stored stress for fuel. The body reawakens and allows us to connect with ourselves in a way that enables an extraordinary wellness and mind-body connection. Network Spinal optimizes our body's abilities to discover what is not energy efficient, to transform into a higher neurological version of ourselves, and to awaken the possibilities of true healing and happiness. Our physical health, emotional response, mental clarity, and DNA expression get an upgrade. It's like upgrading our very own IOS. Our spine finds its proper position of health and wellness naturally on its own, raising our consciousness so we can be our very best.

This to me was proof of how amazing our body, mind, and spirit actually are and was just the miracle I was looking for! I always knew there was more to who we are and the wonder of our true potential. I was all in.

This was the first time I started to conceive that my illness behaviors like depression, ADD, PTSD, addiction behaviors, and anxiety were not because I was weak, lazy, dumb, or gluttonous, but because my over-stressed physical, mental, and emotional body created disconnection as its only defense.

I was in need of a life-changing upgrade, and these new transformational techniques were to be the answer for me and those I was looking to help.

The groundbreaking work of Network Spinal creates entirely new options for living. Through upgrading the neurological system, we achieve a broader bandwidth to stress, which allows us to live happier and healthier lives in all their expressions. This was the path I was destined to follow, the journey I would embark upon to help myself and all of humanity!

Not only was I learning about Network Spinal, but I was also living it. Under Network Spinal care and while practicing SRI exercises, my body and mind took on a new level of expansion. I felt more in sync with my body and more in touch with my authentic self than I ever had in my life! I was experiencing true wellness for the first time. It was incredible. My whole life was opening to me.

I remember a very special morning about six months into care. I was calm, happy, optimistic, and peaceful for no apparent reason. This was not the norm. For my entire life up to this point, I had to push up out of a regular morning depression and anxiety and hope for the best. Now, this emotional and physical armoring was no longer needed. Network and SRI upgraded my neurological system to find greater ease and peace for a healthier life expression, which translated into me waking fresh and optimistic and, most miraculously, not having to check out with food!

I was finally FREE!!! The stress, anger, lack of happiness, feeling unloved, the suicidal tendencies that were always in the shadows were gone. They were finding resolution. I was freeing myself of the self-abuse, shame, and self-loathing prison which practically any disorder can bring. My entire life shifted. I was becoming who I was destined to be. I found a way to help myself heal and set out on the path of providing this service for others now with the courage of knowing who I was, now fueling who I am to become.

• • • • •

I am very proud of myself as I became the first doctor and first business owner in our family's history. I graduated in 2005, with a bachelor's degree in anatomy and a doctorate in chiropractic from Parker University in Dallas, Texas.

Since then, I have traveled worldwide, honing and practicing my craft while studying and mentoring with Dr. Epstein. I chose to stay in Texas, settling in Austin, where I have brought my gifts to the world through my Network Spinal practice, Somato Respiratory Integration Wellness Coaching, and Applied Clinical Nutrition practice at Happiness Chiropractic and Wellness for close to 15 years now. I am lovingly known by my patients as Dr. Rose, The Spine Whisperer.

Due to the pioneering efforts of Dr. Epstein, myself, and my other Network colleagues around the world, Network Spinal care technologies are now some of the most sought-after, leading-edge healing modalities on the planet, and are taught and accepted in many colleges and universities worldwide—institutions which had previously banned his work. This gives a new generation of students the opportunity to raise human consciousness though works like this, when years ago it was not possible.

. . . . .

I believe with all my heart and soul that the voice I heard, over 45 years ago, was the divine Universe firmly capturing my attention and guiding me towards a path of great accomplishment and contribution. I am grateful for listening, staying patient, and being devoutly determined to live my purpose.

I continue to have the routine privilege of being an integral part of every one of my patients' evolutions so that they may live their very best version of themselves for themselves, their loved ones, and the world.

## APPLYING THE LESSONS

Below are suggestions I have to cultivate the best version of yourself. This advice will help you to serve both yourself and humanity as you are called to do.

### 1. Never give up on yourself or your dreams.

No matter what the circumstances are in your life or what impediments you feel you may have, never, ever give up on yourself or your dreams. Trust that whatever inside you feels wounded actually holds a special gift of wisdom for you to receive. Allow yourself the grace of taking time to feel the feelings that are inside of you and move through them, so that you can see the gifts and lessons that your history hold for you.

## 2. Don't go at it alone.

Seek out books, recordings, and podcasts of inspiration and accomplishment by women that you admire who are living the life you desire. Find practitioners, coaches, mentors, friends, and a community of like-minded social and business groups that can help you find your path to your greatest version of you. Women's groups are also a great way to get and stay inspired through sisterhood and bonding.

## 3. Be open to both the unexpected and the unusual.

Life is full of miracles, if you're open to them. Work on cultivating a life that allows for them to appear by getting quiet, turning off your computer, putting down your phone, and getting out into the fresh air of nature. Find practices that quiet the mind and open your consciousness to the most divine version of you to manifest. Create daily practices that connect you with your inner rhythms, authentic expression, and soul purpose. Use dance, song, journaling, drawing, painting, or any other form of creativity that allows your unique gifts to have space to reveal themselves.

## 4. Set boundaries.

Surround yourself with like-minded people and those that are on a growth trajectory of your chosen path. We are all the sum of the five closest people in our lives, so choose wisely, and let go of whoever does not serve your highest and best good. There are many versions of letting such people go and still keeping connected, so find your boundaries that serve your greatness.

## 5. Find what brings you pleasure.

Women thrive on pleasure. Acts done purely for the purpose of pleasure are fuel for the feminine spirit, so always remember to add pleasure into your daily routine. Take a bath with beautiful essential oils, read a fun novel with a wonderful cup of your favorite tea, or get together with your girlfriends for fun and support. One of my favorite authors is Regena Thomashauer (Mama Gena), who has all kinds of wonderful ways to tap into your Goddess self through sisterhood and pleasure. I encourage you to read her one of her books.

Lastly, know that we are all divinely guided, we all have a purpose, and we are all here to share our great purpose with the world. I encourage you to take these suggestions and implement them in your life, because all of these actions will allow the best version of you to shine through you. You are your greatest and most valued resource to yourself, and to the world.

# ready, jet, go!

**TIFFANI MARROQUIN**

Life was great for me at nine years old. That is, until the day I heard the news that my family and I would be moving halfway across the country to Norman, Oklahoma. How could they? I had lived in Virginia since I was three years old, in a yellow two-story home with huge pine trees that touched the clouds. The smell of mint and the purple irises that grew wild added to the beauty of our luscious green yard. In the fall, I loved to collect a variety of leaves in all shades from bright orange and red to brown. Most importantly, it was only a short drive to the ocean. I loved the smell of the salty ocean breeze, the sound of the waves, and the feeling of the sand squishing between my toes. This was where I belonged, not in Oklahoma.

I didn't want to leave my home or my friends. We loved to dance and sing to the latest music videos on MTV. One of our favorite things to do was play hide-and-seek inside new homes being built in the neighborhood. What would I do without my friends? My neighborhood was full of kids, and I feared that my new one wouldn't have children my age. In an instant, my life changed.

As a government employee, my dad applied for and accepted positions from coast to coast. At one point, he landed a five-year gig in Europe. My mom was homesick; they were from a small town in east Texas. Oklahoma was the best option to get her closer to her hometown. We moved into a one-story, four-bedroom brick home that sat on several acres far away from civilization and kids. Being landlocked without a beach in sight was utter torture for me. To top it off, no more true seasons, just two—hot and cold. Why did we move there?! I hated Oklahoma from the minute I heard about it.

To make matters worse, there was no MTV where we lived because we were too far out in the country to get cable service. I didn't like the flat plains, the scorching, sweltering heat, the red dirt, or the fact we lived in tornado alley. I was also a Texas Longhorns fan, and now we lived in the town that was home to their biggest rival—the Sooners!

I felt separated, lost from my herd, and stuck in the dreadful heat of the central plains. The feeling of being seperated made me think of zebras. By nature, zebras are nomadic, social animals that live in herds. Like a fingerprint on a human, the stripes on every zebra are unique, and no two stripes are the same. To me, zebras represent freedom, individuality, and uniqueness, and they're one of the few animals that can't be domesticated. Moving to Oklahoma was, for me, the equivalent of removing a zebra from the wild and placing it in a barnyard--the only zebra among cows and horses. The zebra, I thought, must be my spirit animal.

By middle school, I started liking boys, but few were interested in me. I was taller than most girls and skinny, without any curves. I had a crush on one of the popular boys, who had a great smile and dimples that could melt any girl's heart. The day he asked me to be his girlfriend, I was on cloud nine. The next day, I giddily walked over to him as he stood by his navy blue locker attached to the wall in the slim hallway where all the kids gathered between classes. I slowed as I noticed something a bit off about him. He didn't look happy to see me, as I would expect as a day-old couple. He actually looked a bit distressed. I knew something was wrong. Everyone knew what was about to happen, except for me.

The hall was filled with other students' snickers and laughter, which echoed through the hallway. *What was so funny? Did I miss something?* His gaze darted to the ground as he rested his head on the edge of his locker door. It was hard for him to get the words out, but when he finally spoke, he said, "I can't."

My heart sank. I stared at him in disbelief as he shamefully shook his head. His friends just laughed and pointed at me, creating a roar of laughter down the hallway.

"Ha-ha, she's so flat—what were you thinking?" one of the popular boys blurted out.

In his mind, and in the eyes of his friends, dating me would harm his reputation. I tried to hold back the tears, but I could feel my face turning bright red as my adrenaline spiked, sending my emotions on a roller coaster ride. I spent the entire next class with my head down and my arms folded across my desk. In less than 24 hours, I went from feeling on top of the world to feeling like a worthless scum. This was my first time getting dumped, and my pain was on full display for everyone to witness.

I decided I wasn't good enough to date the popular kids. I was just a tall, skinny weirdo with no curves. As an awkward preteen girl, I didn't have the confidence or the grit to bounce back on my feet. Instead, I went to a deep, dark place, angry at the world. I spent the remaining years of school rebelling, skipping classes, and hanging out with the wrong crowd.

I had a couple of genuine friends who were transplants like me, mostly army brats. We understood one another and shared a special bond that I could never share with the rest of the kids. The kids who grew up together and had never lived in a different city formed a clique, leaving the newbies to fend for ourselves.

One day, my best friend and I were at lunch when a group of six girls asked if we wanted to go for a walk through the neighborhood. It was a beautiful sunny day, and the smell of burgers from a nearby restaurant filled the air. We were halfway down the street when I suddenly felt a hard object hit the back of my head. I lost my balance and fell to the ground. I got a good whiff of freshly cut grass while I tried to make sense of what was happening. Before I could react, I felt a foot to my ribs as I heard laughter coming from the rest of the group. Everyone laughed except my best friend. I could see the pain in her eyes, and she was concerned. She also knew we were outnumbered and couldn't do anything but yell at the other girls to stop. Once my body was thoroughly bruised, they left me alone. I was humiliated. They exchanged high-fives as they laughed uncontrollably and ran back to school. My friend was in just as much shock as I as she helped me stand. I was miserable. My light was gone, and I wished my life as I knew it to end. I had to get out of that place.

That year I attended night classes and had enough credits to graduate early. I hoped to be able to move away for college a year early; however, my parents were never going to let that happen. They feared for my well-being and didn't trust that I would make the best decisions if I were to live away from them. I enrolled in a community college to help the time pass, since I was unable to live out of state.

In 2001, the year I was supposed to graduate high school, I finally moved away. I choose Austin, Texas. It seemed like a fun, cool college town. I liked the slogan "Keep Austin Weird." I felt that I would fit in well. Austin was relatively small back then but still about seven times the size of Norman, which was exciting to me.

Once in Austin, I finally had the freedom I'd craved all those years. And even more importantly, I found my zebras. I met the most amazing bunch of girlfriends, and I fit in nicely with their crowd. I had a knack for meeting people and bringing them together. We took off on weekends to travel, and our trips included Miami, Las Vegas, and Mexico. Our nights dancing to house music from the world's top DJs frequently turned into mornings. I craved the sound of the pounding bass and the unlimited free drinks, likely available due to our skimpy dresses and five-inch heels. My insecurities were now masked by the liquid courage of alcohol and by my newly developed curves.

I felt so liberated, connected, and in love. Most nights were spent drinking, which helped me forget my past and create new memories. I received endless attention from men and soaked it up. In fear of a repeat of my childhood breakup, I never wanted to commit to just one person and wanted to stay in control. My light slowly glimmered back, but it was still heavily poisoned by the fear and mistrust deep within me.

Once I graduated with a business degree, I decided I needed a change of pace, so I moved to Dallas, Texas. My first job catered to retirees who wanted to learn how to invest their money in apartment complexes and single-family homes. As a recent college graduate, I was much younger than my clients. I felt a little out of place, so I decided it was time for me to settle down.

One weekend, I decided to drive down to Austin to enjoy a weekend at the lake. During that weekend, I met a guy who seemed like he had it all together. We were inseparable for the next six weekends before we decided to go party in Las Vegas. While there, we decided it would be fun to get married. Yes, I know—who does that?!

He moved to Dallas with me and supported me through my start of a real estate career as an agent for investors during a recession. A year or so later, I became pregnant with my son, Ethan, which fueled my desire to travel. I wanted him to see the world and be full of happiness and compassion for all cultures. I am a firm believer that traveling is the best education. I also wanted him to know that the world is full of beautiful people and places and to be kind to and accepting of all. I didn't want to raise him in a crappy place or situation.

My husband and I weren't seeing eye to eye, however. We didn't share the same values and goals for life. We ended our marriage, and he moved back to Austin.

I never envisioned myself as a single mom who struggled to make ends meet, especially in my late twenties. Yet I pushed through it and decided to get a corporate job for consistency and comfort. Something felt off, though. This wasn't how my parents raised me.

To be both a father and mother to my son, I knew I had to step up my game. If I wanted to travel with him around the world, I had to work hard, like my dad, and provide the best for my son. I enrolled Ethan in a Spanish immersion preschool and booked our first international trip, to Costa Rica.

I racked up major airline miles and credit card rewards with my new job. I met Danielle, a fellow zebra, on that job. We both knew that we wanted more but weren't quite sure what to do to obtain our goals. I was too scared to go off on my own as a single mom and felt somewhat stuck. One day at the office, as we sat in our little cubicles, we discussed successful entrepreneurs and the dynamics that surrounded them. We decided we were meant for more and filled our heads with knowledge and ideas from books and podcasts, reporting back to each other on our findings. I knew I needed a change, and I needed it in a hurry. I turned into a corporate robot that lacked passion and desire; however, I racked up major credit card points and spent all my free time overseas. I wanted a restart in a different country but ended up back in Austin after an impromptu trip that resulted in me signing a lease. Ethan was about to start kindergarten, and I wasn't sure where to enroll him. Austin was a forward-thinking city, and I felt he would do well there.

I packed up all my things in a U-Haul truck and drove it down to Austin the weekend before Ethan started kindergarten. I felt a sense of belonging and comfort. I felt like I was home, something I hadn't felt since childhood in Virginia. I knew I was on the right track.

I spent the next few years contented at my corporate job, and I worked with real estate investors, helping them to build wealth and grow their businesses. I was back where it all began. This time, however, my territory was nationwide, so it was fun getting to know the different markets. I quickly plateaued, felt stuck, but was afraid to leave a good thing. I had to be able to afford a lifestyle of world travel for my son. Driven to do better, I remembered the words of John D. Rockefeller, "Don't be afraid to give up the good to go for the great!"

After attending an event with Tony Robbins, the master of personal development, I was inspired to find my purpose and shine my light. I had dabbled in an entrepreneurship for many years but never went all in. I realized that was the part of me that was missing.

When I returned home, my negative self-talk jumped into action.

I quickly lost my confidence and felt down on myself. I needed to find more zebras. So I hired a coach named Allyson McGuinty through the Tony Robbins network. She is an accomplished, business-savvy coach who genuinely cares about people and helps them shine bright. After our conversations, I felt empowered and began to believe in my self-worth. Everything standing between me and all that I wanted was myself. It always had been. That's when the words of Paulo Coelho came into play. He said, "When you want something, all the universe conspires in helping you to achieve it." I wanted vacation homes around the world, and I wanted to inspire others to do the same. I created a digital vision board full of the things I desired, and I used it as both my phone and laptop screensavers. I also made a physical version of this vision board and hung it on my wall at home. My bathroom was also full of affirmations and photos.

Two weeks after I set my intentions and shared them with my coach, the company I worked for held an emergency off-site meeting with our executives. We were scheduled to move into our new office the next day, so I found it a bit strange to have all this activity. I pulled up to the Renaissance Hotel in my two-week-old black Mercedes-Benz. I strode into the hotel and spotted some of my coworkers near a large conference room. The room had been decorated with round tables of eight, with crisp white tablecloths for a dining set up. Fresh Starbucks coffee and a small breakfast buffet were set up at the back, with delicious croissants, pastries, omelets, and other items. The room was full of uncertainty and I was confused as to what was about to happen.

The executive started to speak, his voice cracking a bit. He seemed nervous. "What I'm about to tell you is going to affect everyone in this room. We have decided to move all operations out of Austin."

Whoa! The room went completely silent. The energy in the room quickly became stale, as if the air had been sucked away through the vents. Several attendees were in tears, while others were in shock and became worried.

I got chills and felt a sense of excitement, freedom, and a new beginning. To be honest, I felt guilty about responding so positively to the situation. Did I manifest this? Was this really happening? I felt a whole flood of emotions. Fear. Happiness. Freedom. Empowerment. Was this my time to make my move to full-time entrepreneurship? Could I survive on my own, without my steady paycheck?

I had an emergency call with my coach. She reminded me of the intentions and goals I had set and instructed me to trust in the universe. So I did.

I conquered my uncertainty and fear of leaving a steady paycheck. I founded REST Ventures with my coworker, Rhett, with business plan to buy, remodel, and sell real estate. This was something I'd always helped other people do, yet I hadn't done it for myself since the start of my career.

We bought our first investment property the week after our jobs ended. I sold my first million-dollar home and worked on several smaller projects. I knew I was on the right track, but I needed to figure out how to tie in global real estate. Throughout my travels, I'd always checked out real estate investment opportunities. I loved the cobblestone streets and historic homes of Europe, the zen temples of Asia, the laid-back vibe and bungalows of the Caribbean, and the modern skyscrapers of Dubai. I needed to figure out how to make investing in these areas a reality. I realized that to share my knowledge, I had to conquer my fear of public speaking. To be known as the international real estate expert, I had to speak on stage, and I had to be confident in my ability.

My next step included visiting developers in Mexico and Belize, to really understand the markets where Americans would be likely to visit and eventually buy or invest. Once I returned home, I felt confident in my findings and knew it was time to spread the word. I had to speak or I would be doomed to a nine-to-five job for the rest of my life. That thought made me cringe. My inner zebra could not be confined to another endless, grinding schedule.

I was given an opportunity to present my knowledge to 30 fellow investors and agents—and a funny thing happened. Once I arrived, I felt confident, at ease, and excited. That had never happened to me before a speaking engagement.

I took the stage, and I shared my knowledge and my story. It felt amazing to share my passions for travel and real estate and to teach others to do the same. At that moment, my second company, LuxeAbroad, got a major boost. The purpose was to be able to live in luxury for less overseas, to diversify my real estate portfolio to include beautiful places around the world and make memories with friends and family. And now, I'm doing all of that and more.

## APPLYING THE LESSONS

### 1. Identify who you are, inside and out.

No one knows you better than you know yourself, or at least that was what we were all taught. Do you genuinely know yourself inside and out? What drives you? What do you like to do? Answers to these questions should come quickly; yet many people struggle with them. To know yourself inside and out, think about those things you liked to do as a child. What did you want to be when you grew up? I was always fascinated by architecture, luxurious items, high-end fashion, and nature. In some ways, I'm an architect because I'm always finding old, dirty homes and making them prettier. My company, LuxeAbroad, focuses on living in luxury for less by purchasing real estate overseas. Check your search history on your phone or laptop. What are the top sites you visit or things you look up online? Those things are what you're passionate about, what you hold most dear to your heart, and what can point you in the direction of your future career.

"Always remember to follow your heart to find your light." These are the words spoken by my favorite yogi, Alli Bee, after each yoga class.

### 2. Create a vision board and get an accountability partner.

Write down your goals and create a vision board for them. I didn't have any magazines lying around, so I took a screenshot of what I wanted and created an electronic vision board. It was perfect for me because I could set it as my screensaver on my phone and computer. If you're going to go a step further, print it out and hang it on your wall as a constant reminder of your future.

Surround yourself with people who are on the same path as you. Find a mentor or an experienced coach who has had success in business. Two minds coming together create a third consciousness that cannot be attained alone.

## 3. Take action.

Once you create your vision board, take appropriate actions toward reaching your goals. Take immediate action, and go get your future! Don't just talk about it—do it. Set a date for everything you want to create, visualize it daily, look at your vision board, and talk to yourself as though you already have it. Make this your daily morning routine.

Please don't listen to anyone unless you would trade lives with them. Even then, their advice may not be the best for you! The only person who knows what is best for you and your future is you. Learn to trust in your intuition and the feelings in your gut. Pay attention to the road signs of your life; they are everywhere, and you must be open to receive them, or you will miss them. The positive actions you take today lead to your vision board coming to fruition.

## 4. Have fun.

Marc Anthony said, "If you do what you love, you'll never work a day in your life." Dream it, believe it, and have fun with it. If it isn't fun, why are you doing it? Is your current job or business energizing you, or does it deplete you? How do you know? If you fall in love with the process, you're heading in the right direction. If you're always complaining and upset with your life, it may be time for a change.

Take these steps, and you'll become the woman you're meant to be. I encourage you strongly to implement them in your life, and the zebra encourages you to embrace the traits and qualities that make you uniquely you—imperfections and all. Don't be afraid to be yourself and strive to make your mark in the world. If a dorky, insecure kid like me can conquer her fears and step into the woman she needed to be, you can. too! Who cares if you're made fun of, beaten down, or ridiculed? Those who would do so are not your people, and I promise you, there are people out there who are perfect for you.

Let's shine bright together, my loves! Stripes and all. And, just as important, as Jim Rohn reminds us, "If you don't like where you are, move. You are not a tree."

# about the collaborating authors from the society of women entrepreneurs

**Ashley Wainscott** is the founder and CEO of Simply Sold Home Renovations, where she has transformed the residential remodeling industry. Recognized as St. Edward's Entrepreneur of the Year, Ashley took her company from an idea to a million-dollar business. She teaches the importance of self-care while dealing with the challenges of a remodel and all aspects of life. Connect with Ashley on Instagram at @ashleyrwainscott.

**Christin Menendez** left corporate America after a 10-year marketing career to pursue her passion for helping others. She's now an author and self-made love and relationship guru. She helps highly sensitive people heal their broken hearts and move on with their lives so that they can have phenomenal relationships without codependency. Connect with Christin at VirtuousHeality.com.

**Corina Frankie** helps businesses align their communications to provide a better understanding of the needs and motivations of their customers. Her 10-year-old company, Brand Besties, provides experiential marketing services to businesses nationwide. Her personal brand as a trainer and speaker provides people and businesses with the techniques to enhance personal performance in many fields that are particularly relevant in business. Connect with Corina at CorinaFrankie.com and look for her schedule of trainings.

**Deborah Whitby** owns the only woman-owned and operated independent plumbing company in Austin, Texas. She attributes much of her company's success to consistently "minding her money" and having a firm financial foundation in place. In addition to running the plumbing company, she is a Financial Coach who helps women manage their money and keep more of what they make. Connect with Deborah at DeborahWhitby.com.

**Deborah Yager** is an inspirational speaker, coach, and trainer of NLP (Neuro Linguistic Programming), Time Line Therapy®, and hypnosis. She is most passionate about working with women to overcome life's greatest challenges, in order to free them from their false limitations. Connect with Deb and get a complimentary coaching session at YagerTraining.com/WEbook.

**Dr. Denise Simpson** is a master life and leadership coach with a Ph.D. in leadership studies. Denise helps her clients master their inner world to fully realize their mental, emotional, and spiritual potential. Her coaching practice focuses on evidence-based strategies with an emphasis on neuroscience. Join her monthly coaching program, the Deliberate Creators Club. This program combines brain-based strategies with the power of spiritual, metaphysical, and new age principles to help you create a life with intention and purpose. Connect with Denise at DrDeniseSimpson.com.

**Diana Kundrotaite** is working toward a clinical psychology Ph.D. and coaches women who have eating disorders. Connect with Diana Linkedin.com/in/diana-kundrotaite-b3322361.

**Karla Rodriguez** is the host of Metafit Metamind Podcast. On this bilingual podcast, Karla's mission is to normalize the conversation about mental and physical health, giving herself and others a platform to share about their life's journey, join in on the conversation, and connect with others. She has also been a doula, ballroom dancer, crossfit athlete, and of course a new and upcoming writer. Connect with Karla on Instagram at @karlita_xfit_dancer.

**Lita Vallis** is an event planner, educator, artist, and Chloe + Isabel merchandiser who lives in Austin, Texas. She enjoys singing, writing, traveling, and throwing a great themed party. By empowering her family and friends to get together in person as often as possible, Lita fulfills her personal mission to elevate the planet through connection, celebration, and music. Connect with Lita at ChloeAndIsabel.com/Boutique/Lita.

**Rachel Brownlow Lund** is a serial entrepreneur and the founder of Me2Lead, where she coaches and advises women entrepreneurs on business leadership, strategy and power positioning. An Austin Business Journal Profiles in Power award winner, Rachel helps clients grow their income and impact as leaders, entrepreneurs and changemakers. Connect with Rachel on LinkedIn or visit her website at Me2Lead.com.

**Rachel Zierzow** is a healthy living expert, natural foods chef, and culinary instructor. She's on a mission to help people find balance in their lives and find a connection with nature. When she's not in the kitchen, you can find Rachel hiking, swimming, walking her cats, or spending time with family in Austin, Texas. Try out Rachel's recipes, health tips, and online courses at CookLoveHeal.com.

**Dr. Rose Anne Mulligan**, known to many as the "Spine Whisperer," specializes in the leading-edge works of Network Spinal and Somato Respiratory Integration. She is also an applied clinical nutritionist and founder of Happiness Chiropractic and Wellness in Austin, Texas. Dr. Rose has a passion for helping her clients create more joy and abundance in their lives. Her goal is to optimize your physical resilience and resourcefulness, healthy range of emotion, mental clarity, and connected collective consciousness, all through a well aligned spine. Connect with Dr. Rose at HappinessATX.com.

**Tiffani Marroquin** is the founder of LuxeAbroad. She is a global investor, speaker, and REALTOR® with an affinity for world travel and awe-inspiring real estate. She helps adventurous souls purchase real estate overseas to build wealth, create memories, and leave legacies through investing in vacation-homes. Connect with Tiffani for valuable insight into the real estate market and for upcoming retreats and trips around the world at LuxeAbroad.com.

**Connect with these amazing authors all in one place inside The Society of Women Entrepreneurs' Private Facebook Group at Facebook.com/groups/SocietyOf-WE.**

# about the author

## ELLEN SMOAK

**FOUNDER & CEO,
The Society of Women
Entrepreneurs**

Ellen Smoak is a #1 bestselling author, keynote speaker, and entrepreneur who has been called a "true change agent" by Marci Shimoff, star of the hit movie The Secret. Ellen was the keynote speaker at the 2018 TEDx BartonSpringsWomen in Austin, Texas, where her passionate speech, "Confessions of a Former Mean Girl," sparked a call to action for women around the world to learn a better, more empowering way of relating to one another. In her speech, Ellen affirms, "If we're going to keep rising as women, then we absolutely must start treating each other better."

Ellen's passion for women supporting women is informed by her experience, during adolescence, of terrible bullying at the hands of other girls. Experience matched with later insights about this and related problems led Ellen to create The Society of WE. Her inspiring message is perfect for any audience that seeks inspiration and motivation for change.

Ellen has successfully built several six- and seven-figure companies during her 15 years of experience as an entrepreneur. She now spends her time mentoring other businesswomen inside The Society of WE toward greater success, abundance, and prosperity. Connect with Ellen about speaking engagements and watch her TEDx Talk at EllenSmoak.com.

# about the society of women entrepreneurs

**The Society of WE offers community, mentorship, and support to women entrepreneurs worldwide.**

**Our mission is to help *you* achieve *yours*.**

In 2016, the founding members—female entrepreneurs themselves—noticed that most of the training and advice for business-building they came across was geared towards men and failed to take into account the unique challenges and strengths of women entrepreneurs.

They decided to change that.

That summer, they brought together a group of twelve female business owners who were frustrated with the lack of support they had, and The Society of Women Entrepreneurs was born. They met in each other's living rooms twice a month, and within a year, they'd grown to more than 1,500 members.

Today, The Society of WE has thousands of members in multiple cities and is currently expanding to sister chapters nationally and internationally. This ecosystem of women helping, supporting, and mentoring women is attracting new members every day, and The Society of WE is on track to become the most impactful community of women entrepreneurs around the world.

**To support the Society of Women Entrepreneur's movement or learn more about it, visit societyofwe.com.**

# Our Gift to You,
# the Woman Entrepreneur

· · · · ·

## WHETHER YOU'RE JUST STARTING OUT, RUNNING A SIDE-HUSTLE, OR WORKING FULL-TIME IN YOUR BUSINESS...

Research shows that women entrepreneurs deal with different challenges from their male counterparts. And because of this, business building and marketing advice geared towards men just doesn't always work.

## SIMPLY PUT: YOU NEED DIFFERENT ADVICE TO SUCCEED.

We've saved you time and money by putting together some helpful resources specifically for woman entrepreneurs. So take advantage of this *free offer* to access our library of resources to help you grow your business:

# SocietyofWE.com/Free

**(Plus, get a free month of membership!)**